CENTRAL OFFICE OF ARCHITECTURE

CONTEMPORARY
WORLD
ARCHITECTS

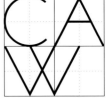

CENTRAL OFFICE OF ARCHITECTURE

Foreword by
Michael Rotondi, FAIA

Introduction by
David Leclerc

Concept and Design by
Lucas H. Guerra
Oscar Riera Ojeda

ROCKPORT PUBLISHERS
GLOUCESTER, MASSACHUSETTS
DISTRIBUTED BY NORTH LIGHT BOOKS
CINCINNATI, OHIO

First published in the United States of America by:
Rockport Publishers, Inc.
33 Commercial Street
Gloucester, Massachusetts 01930-5089
Telephone: (978) 282-9590
Facsimile: (978) 283-2742

Distributed to the book trade and art trade in the United States by:
North Light Books, an imprint of F & W Publications
1507 Dana Avenue
Cincinnati, Ohio 45207
Telephone: (800) 289-0963

Other distribution by:
Rockport Publishers, Inc.
Gloucester, Massachusetts 01930-5089

ISBN 1-56496-407-8
10 9 8 7 6 5 4 3 2 1
Printed in Hong Kong by Midas Printing Limited.

Cover photograph: Brix Restaurant by Tom Bonner. Back cover photographs: (Top) Laguna Beach Residence by Benny Chan, (Bottom) Pacific Palisades Residence by Tom Bonner. Back flap photographs: (Top) Ron Golan, (Center) Eric Kahn, and (Bottom) Russell Thomsen. Pages 1-3 photographs: Brix Restaurant by Tom Bonner

Graphic Design: Lucas Guerra / Oscar Riera Ojeda
Layout: Oscar Riera Ojeda

CONTENTS

Foreword

BY MICHAEL ROTONDI, FAIA

Twentieth-century architecture has been characterized largely by a sensitivity to the context in which it has been practiced. It reflects an exploration of new forms of language, consciousness, and social relationships, brought about by deliberate experimentation in the present and by reinterpretation of the past. As the world we have made moves faster, the cycles of change become increasingly shorter, which suggests that our belief systems should change at the same rate. Maybe they do not do this for everyone. If our focus broadens, time, scale, and cycles can seem to get larger until everything apparently becomes still. History comes to rest. At this moment our gaze across becomes our focus into what we are studying. We go to a depth that has no boundaries or limits; to where the unknown resides. Perhaps this is the quest. At this time of unprecedented social and technological change, what could possibly motivate three architects working in collaboration and integrating their intelligences and skills, to be singularly committed to exploring the problem of architecture (as an artistic and social medium) through the principles of modernism as they have evolved over the last seventy-five years? What remains unexplored? What is the relevance of these principles?

COA, Russell Thomsen, Eric Kahn, and Ron Golan, are continuing the modern project as an unbroken tradition. They practice and teach with such a sincerity and steadfastness that they set an example for their students and colleagues. They have an unyeilding belief that architecture holds great promise for the advancing human endeavor.

The simple, well-lit volume of white plaster walls and concrete floor in the Pacific Palisades Residence (opposite) contrasts with the furniture and steel stair, resulting in a straightforward distinction between the building enclosure and servant objects (equipment). The model of the Dynamic of the Metropolis (left) makes clear the intersection of the different ordering structures that comprise the dense and complex urban fabric of downtown Los Angeles.

Introduction

BY DAVID LECLERC

WHITE BY DEFAULT

THE WORK OF CENTRAL OFFICE OF ARCHITECTURE

One image symbolizes the project of Central Office of Architecture: a man, walking on a flat desert, carries on his shoulders the Villa Savoye of Le Corbusier. Detached from the ground, the white villa loses its physical quality and becomes the embodiment of a set of architectural principles. Titled "Atlas Modernism," this collage by COA questions our relationship to the heroic period of the Modern Movement. The man is far away from the original arcadian site where he found his icon and has reached the limit of the desert.

Central Office of Architecture believes that the project of Modern Architecture is not dead. COA's three principals, Ron Golan, Eric A. Kahn, and Russell N. Thomsen, met while students at the California Polytechnic State University in San Luis Obispo, where they graduated in 1981. After several years of professional experience in Europe and the United States, they established Central Office of Architecture in 1987 in Los Angeles. Their office works on both built and theoretical work, as well as teaching architectural design studio at the Southern California Institute of Architecture (SCI-Arc) and Woodbury University.

For the past decade, COA's *recherche* has been *patiente*, conducted in an environment often hostile to the ideas of modern architecture. But this long and sometimes lonely journey has also offered the framework in which their work has matured. COA's built work is so far limited to domestic architecture and the remodeling of existing buildings. The lack of access to larger commissions, experienced by most emerging architects in Los Angeles, did not prevent COA from exploring larger urban, architectural, and ideological issues through a series of theoretical urban projects, furniture designs, written manifestos, and publications. The work presented in this book illustrates both the coherence of COA's ideas and the open nature of its search as it evolves through time.

Many contemporary West Coast architects found in the chaotic urban environment of Los Angeles a source of inspiration to reconsider the formal constituency of their architecture. But too often the desire for self-expression and originality (being the *avant-garde à tout prix*) led to the production of egocentric objects, devoid of any urban or humanistic agenda, more concerned for making the covers of architectural magazines than serving the needs of the city and its inhabitants. This formal exuberance is often a means to assert the presence of the architectural object in an increasingly congested visual environment. The rise of media-culture and a long tradition of simulacra nurtured by Hollywood's movie industry, tend to reduce architecture to a packaging problem, to the advertising of corporate public images, or to a private frivolous object more concerned with its sculptural proficiency than its ability to celebrate the joy of living. This desire for personal expression and "authored" architecture, which has long been one of the hallmarks

of Los Angeles's multiple identities and eclectic urban environment, is condemned by COA both as a decadent set of values for architecture and as one of the causes of the decay of the urban structure. COA sees its work as the continuation of an unfinished project, as in the development of a type, established by the founders of the European modern movement in the early 1920s with its roots in the Age of Enlightenment. While Frank Gehry is often (and mistakenly) presented as the godfather of the so-called "Los Angeles School," in COA's work Le Corbusier plays the role of godfather. His influence is not disguised, but on the contrary fully acknowledged, sometimes even with humor. Le Corbusier's architectural legacy is also the subject of an ongoing case study in COA's design studios at SCI-Arc. For COA, Le Corbusier's five points of architecture, his "Modulor," the idea of function as a driving force in the making of architecture, the figure of the architect as both poet and engineer, are still vital.

The strength of the modern architectural movement in Southern California came from its ability to understand the "genius loci," to absorb a vernacular culture of construction, and finally to adapt its social and ideological agenda to serve and enhance a local tradition of living. Unfortunately, this rich legacy was quickly forgotten. A program such as the Case Study House, during the post–World War II era, intended to promote the ideas of modern architecture in single-family housing, remained a marginal enterprise and had very little influence in the production of everyday architecture.

While COA more often refers to the European modern movement as a source for their work, the works of some practitioners of modern architecture in Southern California have been influential as well. Aside from the romantic and highly personal vision of modernism found in the work of Rudolph Schindler and the more literal interpretation of the International Style illustrated by the work of Richard Neutra, the work of Gregory Ain, a lesser-known figure from the second generation, presents interesting parallels with COA's ideas. In a letter written in 1973, Ain noted that his architectural designs were "… always intended to be a precise solution to prior stated problems, rather than Architecture; inevitably [it] has far less 'eye-appeal' than contemporary work which may have had a different motivation. The camera has never been part of my problem."[1]

Union Terminal Warehouse, Los Angeles (opposite). Anonymous architecture provides a lesson in structural, urbanistic, and material response to a clearly stated problem. The result is striking both in expression and as an unselfconscious tool. "Atlas Modernism," montage by COA (above left). Unité d'Habitation (above right), an exhibition of modern architecture organized by COA at the Southern California Institute of Architecture (SCI-Arc) in 1996.

Ain's remark points out precisely what COA criticizes in the Los Angeles School, an architecture more interested in "eye-appeal" than being, as Le Corbusier described the automobile design of his time, a solution to "a problem which has been well stated."[2] Ain's interest in low-cost housing both as a generator of urban fabric and as a social agenda, are regarded by COA as a model in the conception of the contemporary city. His Dunsmuir Flats of 1937 and Mar Vista Housing for Advanced Development, built in 1946–1948, are still, half a century later, surprisingly visionary compared to the mass-produced tract houses built today all over California in Spanish colonial and French chateaux styles.

Ideas for a City

While some have looked at Los Angeles's chaotic urban environment as an exhilarating force for the making of architecture, others have underlined the decay of its urban structure, its complete disregard for public urban spaces, and its increasingly segregated, introverted and armed-controlled environment. From Reyner Banham's and Jean Baudrillard's[3] poetic mapping of Los Angeles's urban palimpsest to the recent dystopian and alarming portrait traced by Mike Davis in his book *City of Quartz*, the city is still today, as Bertolt Brecht had once described it, the simultaneous incarnation of the paradise and the inferno.

Los Angeles is a complex composite of urban structures and infrastructures over which is laid an unstable and constantly shifting mosaic of ethnic groups and social patterns. The absence of a consistent direction for growth and development has transformed what was originally an Arcadia into what many see today as an urban nightmare. The endless reproduction of the American dream, the single-family house on its private lot, and rapid urban growth driven by mere speculation and real estate profit, has led the city to a point of collapse, as illustrated by the recent riots.

A keen eye is missing. The economic exploitation of the city, along with "rampant frontierism," encourage the continual shedding of the area's morphological structure. An inspired interpretation of Los Angeles leads one to realize that a viable and complex urbanism exists. Its structure and potential, however, have been undermined by neglect, by recent decades of accelerated shifts in demographics, and by blind, insensitive growth.[4]

COA's theoretical urban proposals question the idea of plurality and chaos as freedom. Architecture, by definition, strives for legibility and order, and therefore is a means of resistance against the increasing entropy of the modern metropolis. Acknowledging the hybrid nature of the city as a set of individual structures, each responding to a particular set of circumstances, COA's projects seek to increase the legibility of each of these parts and the relationships between them. Two different approaches characterize COA's interventions. When an underlying structure already exists, the project will reinforce it to amplify the existing condition. This first strategy is exemplified in their proposal, Divining Underlying Structure: Los Angeles and the Curse of Bigness, which explores two different areas of downtown Los Angeles. The one called the Object Zone is typical of American downtown urban development since the 1960s, in which the buildings, mostly towers and slabs, become objects in a field. The postmodern architectural and urban culture, dominant in the 1980s, strongly rejected the nature of these urban spaces, and in their place promoted pastiches of past architectural styles to bring down the scale of the high-rises' facades and pompous stage-set clichés of traditional urban

Mar Vista Housing for Advanced Development, Los Angeles, Ain, Johnson and Day, Architects, built from 1946 to 1948. The architects sought to design low-cost, mass-produced housing types in response to the needs of the postwar family.

space to celebrate the power of American corporations. COA's proposal, on the contrary, acknowledges the potential of this contemporary condition for the making of a new type of urban experience. Noticing that the high-rise typology generates a disintegration of the street edge, the project proposes to amplify this existing condition and simply to erase the reading of the urban grid in the area. A plinth acts as a substitute ground plane to reinforce the nature of the zone as a random dispersion of objects. It organizes the area programmatically (it houses all service functions for the buildings above, including parking) while allowing on its free surface an urban experience that results between objects.

In the second approach, an existing urban structure, seen as deficient or obsolete, is replaced by a new one. In their housing project, Re: American Dream, COA is not afraid of using the modernist "tabula rasa" as the point of departure for their project. By simply replacing the existing single-family houses and their property lines by new typologies of row housing, the project is able to compare, with a "Hilberseimer-like" scientific rigor, the existing condition with the proposed one. Under the slogan "Densify or Die," the Re: American Dream proposal offers new alternative types to the spatially wasteful current typology of detached single-family houses on their private lots. By modifying zoning codes, set-back requirements, and circulation patterns, the project demonstrates the possibility of increasing the current density of a residential block by more than two and one-half times without sacrificing any of the assets of the American dream: land ownership, individual home, private outdoor space, and private garage. COA strongly believes in the idea of living in the city and in the value of the type as the generator of urban fabric; but it condemns what has been seen by many as the essence of the Los Angeles lifestyle—the artificial stylistic differences that characterize the housing stock in the city.

The idea of densifying Los Angeles's residential urban fabric goes back as far as the early 1920s, with Spanish colonial courtyard housing, Irving Gill's apartment courts, and the multi-unit residential projects designed by Rudolph Schindler, Richard Neutra, and Gregory Ain in the 1930s. Unlike most typologies of housing developed since World War II, such as the infamous mass-produced dingbats, which were driven by quick real estate profit and cheap imagery, all the above were deeply concerned with creating new housing types that offered alternatives to the detached single-family house on its private lot, while respecting the essence of the American dream. They all strived to reconcile privacy and community. COA's Re: American Dream proposal is rooted in this enduring tradition.

From Object to Tool

An evolution can be traced in COA's work of the last decade, from a purely formal exploration of architectural ideas to a more utilitarian conception of architecture as a tool. In their 1986 project The Absolute and Autonomous Object, COA explored the sculptural nature of a series of abstract formal compositions and the transformation of their cast shadows in search of a formal language. But these

Dynamic of the Metropolis, overview (above left). Re: American Dream, Los Angeles (above right). View of the project showing the new public park in the foreground, with the housing units beyond. "Measurement, Experiment, and Production," collage by COA (opposite).

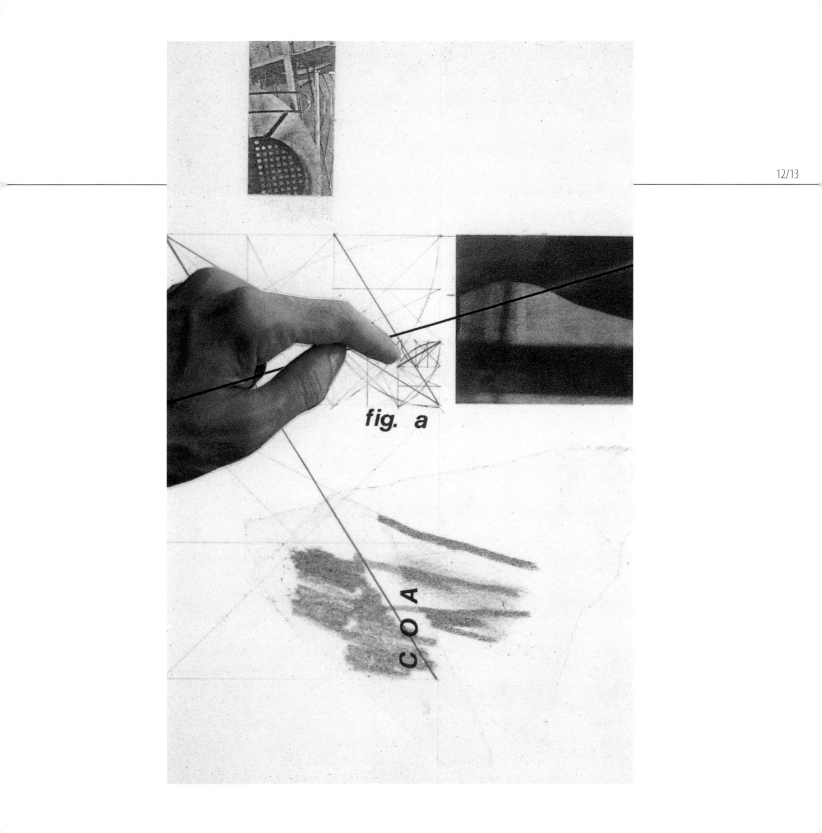

fig. a

C O A

artifacts are consciously presented as ideas about architecture and not buildings, because they are intentionally designed without program and use. A similar emphasis is present in their astonishing model for the "Object Zone" of downtown Los Angeles. The desire to create a utopian framework in which pure architectural issues can be freely explored and addressed without the requirements and limitations of the real world, masterfully exemplified in the 1920s work of the Russian avant-garde by Leonidov, Chernikhov, and Malevich, is essential in COA's architectural practice.

This intuitive search in the realm of form goes along with a desire to reestablish a set of values and rational criteria for the making of architecture and to reassert, as Adolf Loos did once, the importance of the distinction between a work of art and an article of use. Without denying the role of architecture as an object of contemplation, COA's recent work explores the nature of architecture as a tool, a machine that solves a problem. For COA, the tool is a means while the object is an end. The tool creates the object, therefore the quality of the object should derive from the efficiency of the tool. The house built by Charles and Ray Eames in Pacific Palisades in 1949 represents the embodiment of this line of thought— an architecture not aesthetically self-conscious, in which form and therefore the aesthetic are not imposed or applied, but spring simply from the coherence and legibility of its constructional system.

The idea that function is again the guiding principle of architecture recalls the old controversial modernist equation of "form follows function." To avoid the reductive approach of the Functionalists of the 1930s, of an architecture driven by merely utilitarian needs, COA proposes a new "humanist functionalism" that expands the definition of function in architecture. Function, seen as a guiding principle for the making of architecture, is not an end in itself, but a means to enable other ends: The project of a tool-architecture is without determinism (it enables); the "machine à habiter" poses new conditions but no more determines how life will be lived than the "machine à écrire" determines what will be written.[5]

Pipes: typology study (above). "Sliding Towards Extinction" exhibition at the California Academy of the Sciences in San Francisco, 1988 (opposite). Design by Whitney Lowe with COA as design consultant.

This concern for a tool-architecture is already present in the Brix Restaurant of 1991, in which a billboard structure is used as a preexisting piece of engineering adapted to fulfill the specific needs of the project, a fast-food restaurant on a commercial strip. Hovering between the street and the remodeled building, the imposing structure and its perforated-metal screen act simultaneously as a signal to identify the fast-food restaurant in the highly congested visual environment of the strip, as a shading device for the glass-box dining room located behind it, as a shield to protect the interior of the dining room from the visual chaos of the exterior, and finally as a threshold to mark the entrance into the parking lot. The ability to solve several architectural problems with one single element validates the choice of the billboard as a tool. But the most unexpected aspect of the Brix Restaurant is that the economy of means and this "problem-solving" type of process produce such a poetic artifact. The encounter between the wood-frame box and

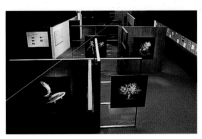

the billboard, not unlike a surrealist "cadavre exquis," reveals the ephemeral (weak) nature of architecture in Los Angeles when confronted with the overwhelming presence of the cantilevered billboard structure that exhibits its huge steel pipes and welded connections like the taut muscles of a body builder.

The Janczak-Jaeckel residence, or Maison Outil (House Tool), an addition to an existing house in the San Fernando Valley, is designed to be as tool-like as possible. Three discrete programmatic volumes are interlocked to create a sequence of new spaces off the existing house. Le Corbusier's Modulor is used as a tool to control the proportional relationship between these three pieces and their relationship to human scale. The articulation of the enclosure opposes large solid walls for privacy to the west and the south with continuous glass walls to open the interior spaces onto the outdoor court, fulfilling the client needs of privacy. The resolution of the programmatic requirements in platonic elementary volume, reveals COA's desire for legibility, coherence, and harmony, clearly apart from contemporary formal addictions to complexity, fragmentation, wrapping, and folding. When asked why the volumes of the Janczak-Jaeckel residence are white, COA explains that it is not a stylistic decision—white as a trademark of modern architecture—but rather a choice by default. White for them is the simplest solution in the absence of any reason to make it otherwise.

By returning to the very ideological core of the European modern movement, COA clearly takes a stand against the tendencies of current architecture to blur the boundaries between art and architecture, form and content, substance and appearance, subjectivity and objectivity. COA views the state of contemporary culture as decadent and irresponsible; yet it is within this very crisis that COA's project finds its purpose.

Modern Architecture cannot live if limited to a pure rhetorical language, an aesthetic goal, a style to make white fashionable objects for the elite. The essence of this project is still a humanistic quest to serve the most profound needs of human life. COA's work is a vivid testimony that this quest is alive and that in a world increasingly confused and unstable, architecture is a means to understand the foundation of our existence as human beings.

1. Letter of Gregory Ain to David Gebhard dated July 24, 1973. From *The Architecture of Gregory Ain* (UCSB Art Museum, 1980).
2. Le Corbusier, *Towards a New Architecture* (Dover, 1986): 4.
3. See Jean Baudrillard, *Amerique* (1986) and Reyner Banham, *The Architecture of Four Ecologies* (1971).
4. Central Office of Architecture, "Divining Underlying Structure: Los Angeles and the Curse of Bigness," *Offramp* Vol. 1, No. 2 (SCI-Arc, 1989).
5. See Stanford Anderson, "The Fiction of Function," *Assemblage 2* (Cambridge, Massachusetts: MIT Press, 1986).

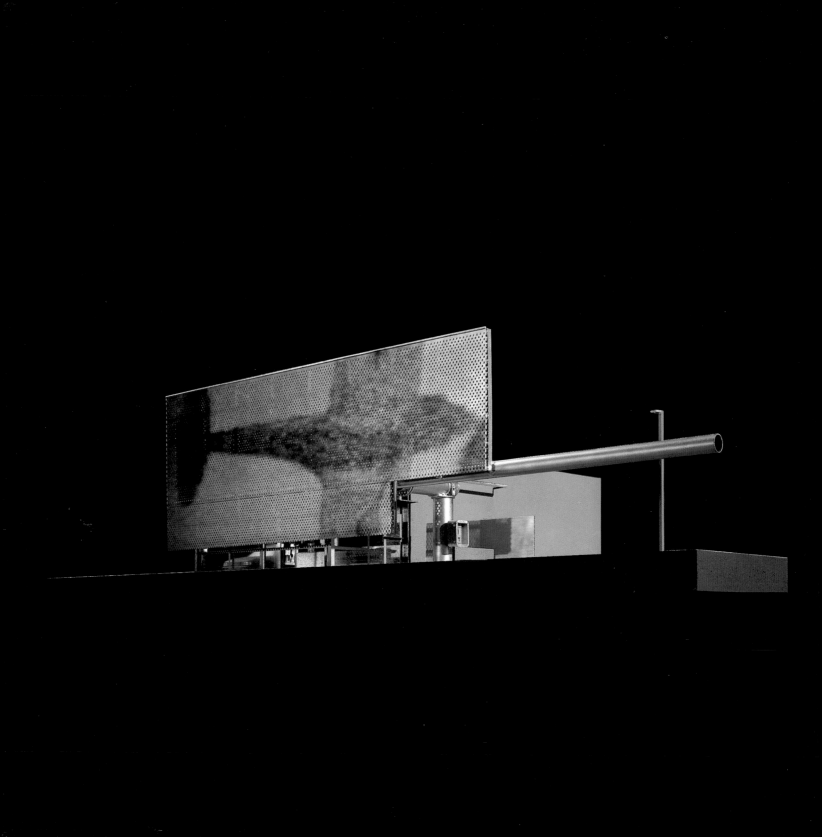

Works ▶

The Absolute and Autonomous Object

From their first collaborations, the principals of COA realized that the task of architecture was one of establishing a relatedness between things. Too many of the projects by other architects seemed to them unrelated to anything, insular unto themselves. In response, these first improvisations were an exploration into the nature of relationships both inside and outside the object, parts to the whole, horizontal to vertical, object to horizon, and three-dimensional form to its silhouette. As a result of this collaborative exercise, communal rules and intentions regarding order, structure, and hierarchy began to emerge.

The "objects" are each experiments in order, structure, hierarchy, the establishment of rules, and their violation. The importance of this project did not reside in the resulting external forms, but in the development and understanding of a strong, underlying order that would be the basis for future work.

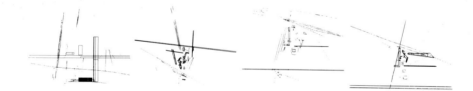

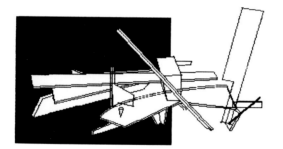

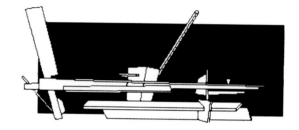

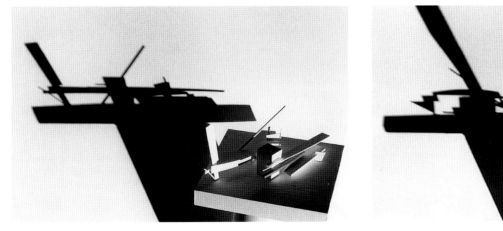

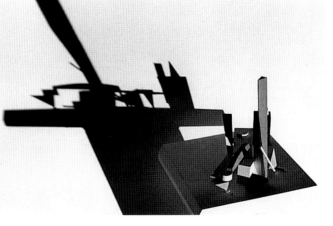

Recombinant Images

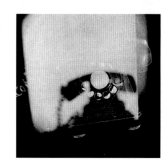

THE COLLAPSE OF EXPERIENCE

The historical precedent for recombinance is found in the twentieth-century avant-garde. For the avant-garde, the metropolis served as the raw material and specific site where instantaneous and radiating events set up the possibility for a new experiential field. The metropolis seen as total theater,[1] simultaneously violent and poetic, gave birth to the idea of the hybrid man-machine, which played the dual role of the city's constructor and slave.

A heuristic logic evolved out of this new amplified-urbanism in response to the ever increasing fragmentation and decentering of culture and the concurrent loss in axiomatic meaning. The avant-garde's development of the collage and the superimposed image, ostensibly to reintegrate art back into the praxis of life, became the method of exposing and ultimately proposing the emerging new world. An additional item on the avant-garde's agenda was the desire to deprecate the institution of art itself and to remove the artist from the production-consumption cycle in an attempt to be free from the bondage of art's self-referential status in bourgeois society.[2]

Moholy-Nagy's first and most important film script, *Dynamic of the Metropolis*, written in the early 1920s and first published in Massachusetts in 1924, became a pivotal piece in his attempt to unite all the avant-garde tendencies into the total *Gesamtskunstwerk*.[3] The film script itself includes a variety of images depicting the life of the metropolis: industrial installations and highways, and various diagrams exhibiting movement, direction, and modulation. These images are placed together with a text to form *Typophotos* structurally reminiscent of Dada poetry:

> Building construction with an iron crane
> Use of special trick effects—line drawings—melting
>   slowly into the filming of nature.
> Crane for construction:
>   shot from below
>   diagonally
> from above
> elevator for bricks
> revolving crane

As it stands in its final configuration, a film script such as this one is very closely related to the photomontage, as images from different time periods and verbal descriptions of disparate events are collaged into a unity in which everything is presented simultaneously rather than chronologically.[4]

RECOMBINANT IMAGES

The camera as a machine-eye registers a series of images. The scrambled syntax implied by these images radically breaks the normative praxis of linear single-image cognition. The smooth space of the recombinant image acts as a collector and homogenizer of all events allowing for the coexistence of the possible with the impossible. These images embrace chance and the found object for their absolute aesthetic absenteeism,[5] but more importantly their purpose is to unveil the metropolis in a complex and simultaneous manner proper to its character. From the production-aesthetic point of view they depend on the superimposition of found urban artifacts pulled from their functional context and treated as "fragment" and empty sign. As analogical constructs they posit a virtually collapsed space-time synonym, becoming both appearance and apparition. Paradoxically, the effect is that of a real scene, a synopsis of actions, produced by originally unrelated space-and-time elements that demand reconciliation. Ultimately they are quite unstable images.

Duchamp's coinage of the term *inframince*, the combination of two French words, the prefix infra (under) and an adjective mince (thin), in English becomes *infrathin*.[6] For Duchamp, the meaning of the word "thin" is stretched to accommodate a multitude of spatial, erotic, and metaphysical phenomena. In his own words describing The Large Glass: "Painting on glass seen from the unpainted side gives an infrathin." We can assume that *infrathin* means not only physical thinness, but signifies a plane of interference and/or simultaneity in communication(s) where phenomena are subjected to various recombinant forces.

> Kind of Sub-Title
> Delay in Glass instead of "picture" or
> "painting"; "picture on glass" becomes
> "delay in glass"-but "delay in
> glass"-does not mean "picture
> on Glass."[7]

The recombinant image collapses content, space, and time into a single photograph that documents and explores conditions of the contemporary metropolis.

The superimposed layers of the recombinant image share the similar "thinness" of Duchamp's infrathin. These layers exist in a collapsed (discontinuous) space and time, that unstable plane where disparate elements coexist. Phenomenally, this collapse results in the compression of experience; experience that has been erased in the final image except for its traced memory, understood as that which is the in between the between.

Karlheinz Stockhausen's *musique concrète* opus, *Hymnen*, composed in 1966 at the WDR Studio for electronic music, incorporates the phonic "ready-made." As with Duchamp, Stockhausen depends on the latent meaning of the found object and its reuse in a

new context to posit new meaning. Stockhausen divides *Hymnen* into four separate pieces. Each of the four center around a specific set of national anthems and each is dedicated to a specific musician (Boulez, Pousseur, Cage, and Berio).[8] In addition to national anthems, further found sounds, such as recordings of public events, recorded conversations, sounds from shortwave radios, demonstrations, the christening of a ship, a Chinese store, and a diplomatic reception have been used. Restructured and modulated by electronics, sound or "noise" in the most basic sense (now standard fare in techno-scratch music) and fragments of the spoken word become the basic raw material for the piece itself.

When one integrates known music with unknown new music in a composition, one can hear especially well how it was integrated: untransformed, more or less transformed, transposed, modulated, etc. The more self-evident the WHAT, the more attentive the listener becomes to the HOW.

> Hide what you compose in what you hear.
> Cover what you hear.
> Place something next to what you hear.
> Place something far away from what you hear.
> Support what you hear.
> Continue for a long time an event you hear.
> Transform an event until it becomes unrecognizable.
> Transform an event that you hear into the one you composed last.
> Compose what you expect to come next.
> Compose often, but also listen for long periods to what is already composed, without composing.
> Mix all these instructions.
> Increasingly accelerate the current of your intuition.[9]

1. Kristina Passuth, *Moholy Nagy* (New York: Thames and Hudson, 1985): 45.
2. Ibid.
3. Peter Burger, *Theory of the Avant Garde* (Minneapolis: University of Minnesota Press, 1984): 53.
4. Joseph Caton, *The Utopian Vision of Moholy-Nagy* (Michigan: UMI Research Press, 1984): 79.
5. Madrid 1984 exhibition catalogue to Duchamp Retrospective, Fundacio Joan Miro, p. 176.
6. Ibid. Yoshiaki Tono, Duchamp and "Inframince," p. 54.
7. A typographic version by Richard Hamilton of Marcel Duchamp's *Green Box, The Bride Stripped Bare By Her Bachelors, Even* (New York: Jaap Rietman Inc., 1976).
8. Robin Maconie, *The Works of Karlheinz Stockhausen* (London: Marion Boyars and Oxford University Press, 1976): 21.
9. Karlheinz Stockhausen, Liner Notes to *Hymnen* (Electronic and concrete music).

Pacific Palisades Residence

Confronted with an example of the typical suburban tract house, COA established the need to occupy the site more efficiently while redistributing the program more sensitively. The typical residential 50 feet x 150 feet (15 meters x 45 meters) lot has a distant view of the Pacific Ocean to the south and the Santa Monica Mountains to the north. The 2,000-square-foot (180-square-meter) program includes new living, sleeping, and bathing areas. Additional elements include a new garage and darkroom.

The addition is conceived simultaneously as an absolute and autonomous object and as a projection of the underlying geometry of the existing residence. The site then becomes a potential assemblage of distinct pieces accumulated over time, all relating to the existing one-story stucco residence. The existing house acts figuratively as a found archaeological object, laden with the presence of memory deposited by previous owners and the clients' own thirty-five years of habitation.

The intervention cuts surgically into the existing house, revealing its geometry, spatial types, and relations to the site. The addition incorporates new living and sleeping areas, positioned for light and view. Vacated spaces in the existing residence are reprogrammed with home offices and a darkroom. Most of the program is located in a two-story concrete-block volume at the rear of the site. An open living area occupies the first floor; the new master bedroom is upstairs. Two service towers frame a sky-lit hallway connecting the existing residence to the addition. At the front of the site, a new metal-clad garage creates a private courtyard entry, screening the house from the noise of the street.

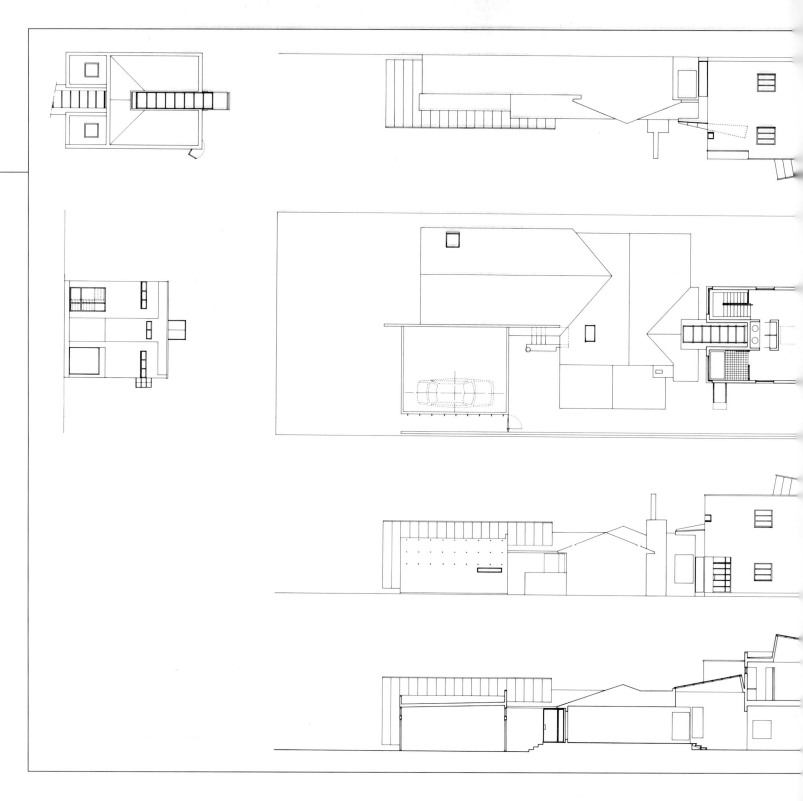

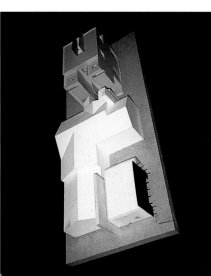

Plans, sections, and elevations indicating the disposition of program elements (opposite). The service entrance is located along the side yard where the new addition meets the existing house (above). Two preliminary sketches show the relationship of the new building to nature (center). Massing model showing the general disposition of building volumes on the site (bottom).

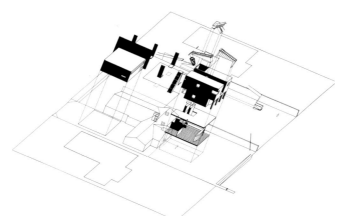

A new entry courtyard/outdoor dining area is formed by the placement of the new garage in relation to the existing house (above). Exploded axonometric view catalogues the building elements (center). View from the street to the new garage (bottom). Detail drawings of the various steel fabrications (opposite).

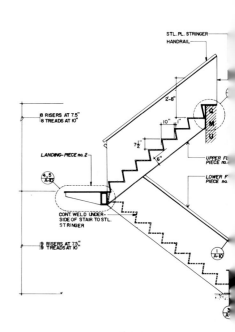

STL.PL. STRINGER
HANDRAIL

2'-8"

8 RISERS AT 7.5"
8 TREADS AT 10"

10"

7½"

LANDING- PIECE no. 2

UPPER FL
PIECE no.

6"

4,5
A-10

LOWER F
PIECE no.

CONT. WELD UNDER-
SIDE OF STAIR TO STL.
STRINGER

9 RISERS AT 7.5"
9 TREADS AT 10"

1
A-10

3
A-

STAIR SECTION   ½" = 1'-0"

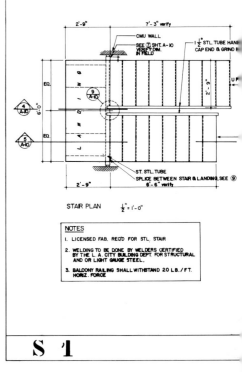

2'-9"   7'-3" verify

CMU WALL
SEE 7/ SHT. A-10
VERIFY DIM.
IN FIELD

1½" STL. TUBE HAND
CAP END & GRIND

EQ.

9
A-10

2'-9"

U

4
A-10   6'-0"

5
A-10   EQ.

ST. STL. TUBE
SPLICE BETWEEN STAIR & LANDING, SEE 9

2'-9"   6'-6" verify

STAIR PLAN   ½" = 1'-0"

NOTES
1. LICENSED FAB. REQ'D FOR STL. STAIR

2. WELDING TO BE DONE BY WELDERS CERTIFIED
   BY THE L. A. CITY BUILDING DEPT. FOR STRUCTURAL
   AND OR LIGHT GAUGE STEEL.

3. BALCONY RAILING SHALL WITHSTAND 20 LB./FT.
   HORIZ. FORCE

S 1

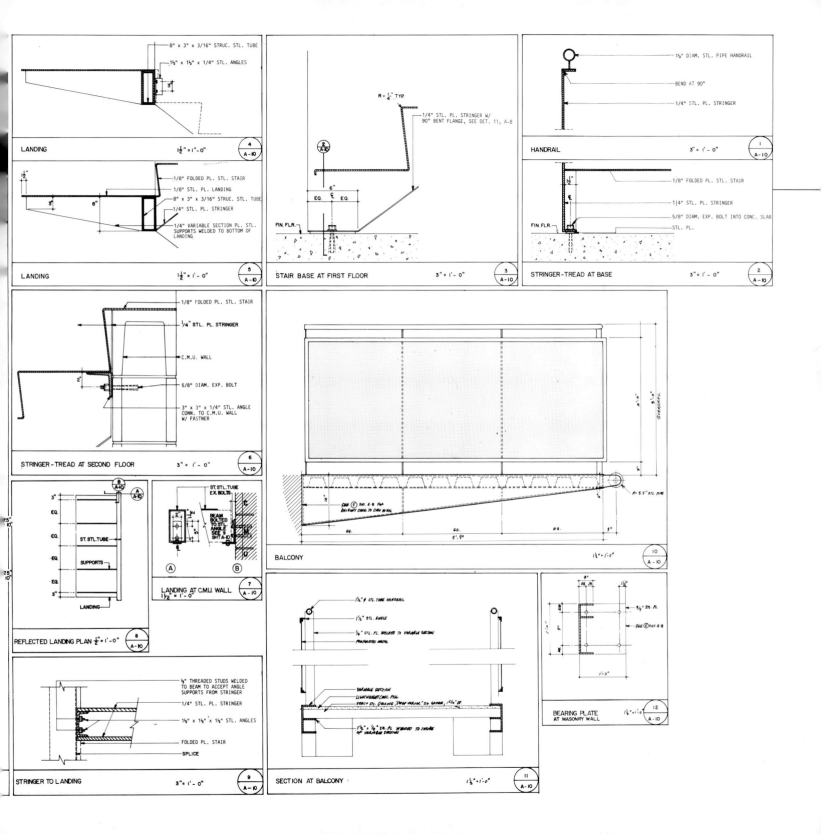

LANDING   1½" = 1'-0"   4 / A-10

8" x 3" x 3/16" STRUC. STL. TUBE
1½" x 1½" x ¼" STL. ANGLES

LANDING   1½" = 1'-0"   5 / A-10

1/8" FOLDED PL. STL. STAIR
1/8" STL. PL. LANDING
8" x 3" x 3/16" STRUC. STL. TUBE
1/4" STL. PL. STRINGER
1/4" VARIABLE SECTION PL. STL. SUPPORTS WELDED TO BOTTOM OF LANDING

STAIR BASE AT FIRST FLOOR   3" = 1'-0"   3 / A-10

R = ¼" TYP
1/4" STL. PL. STRINGER W/ 90° BENT FLANGE, SEE DET. 11, A-8
2 / A-10
6"
EQ. C EQ.
FIN. FLR.

HANDRAIL   3" = 1'-0"   1 / A-10

1½" DIAM. STL. PIPE HANDRAIL
BEND AT 90°
1/4" STL. PL. STRINGER

STRINGER-TREAD AT BASE   3" = 1'-0"   2 / A-10

1/8" FOLDED PL. STL. STAIR
1/4" STL. PL. STRINGER
5/8" DIAM. EXP. BOLT INTO CONC. SLAB
STL. PL.
FIN. FLR.

STRINGER-TREAD AT SECOND FLOOR   3" = 1'-0"   6 / A-10

1/8" FOLDED PL. STL. STAIR
1/4" STL. PL. STRINGER
C.M.U. WALL
5/8" DIAM. EXP. BOLT
3" x 3" x 1/4" STL. ANGLE CONN. TO C.M.U. WALL W/ FASTNER

REFLECTED LANDING PLAN ½" = 1'-0"   8 / A-10

ST. STL. TUBE
SUPPORTS
LANDING

LANDING AT C.M.U. WALL   1½" = 1'-0"   7 / A-10

ST. STL. TUBE EX. BOLTS
BEAM BOLTED TO STL. ANGLE SEE 5 SHT. A-10
A   B

BALCONY   1½" = 1'-0"   10 / A-10

SEE F SHT. A-8 FOR BALCONY CONN. TO C.M.U. WALL
R = 3.5" STL. PIPE
EQ.   EQ.   EQ.   3"
5'-9"

STRINGER TO LANDING   3" = 1'-0"   9 / A-10

½" THREADED STUDS WELDED TO BEAM TO ACCEPT ANGLE SUPPORTS FROM STRINGER
1/4" STL. PL. STRINGER
1½" x 1½" x 1½" STL. ANGLES
FOLDED PL. STAIR
SPLICE

SECTION AT BALCONY   1½" = 1'-0"   11 / A-10

1½" ⌀ STL. TUBE HANDRAIL
1½" STL. ANGLE
1/8" STL. PL. WELDED TO VARIABLE SECTION
PERFORATED METAL
VARIABLE SECTION
LIGHTWEIGHT CONC. FILL
VERCO STL. DECKING "DURA WALL" 26 GAUGE, 1½" DP.
1½" x 1/8" STL. PL. WELDED TO INSIDE OF VARIABLE SECTION

BEARING PLATE AT MASONRY WALL   1½" = 1'-0"   12 / A-10

3/4" STL. PL.
SEE 6 SHT. A-8
1'-0"

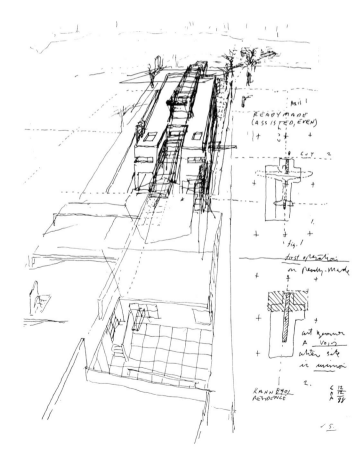

The interior spaces are visually continuous from the dining room to the living spaces, implying an extension into the garden beyond. The divisions between rooms are marked by skylights and changes in level.

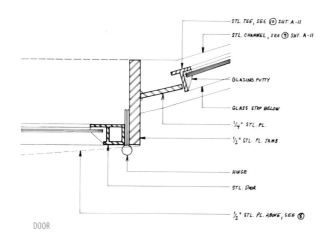

DOOR

STL. TEE, SEE ⑩ SHT. A-11
STL. CHANNEL, SEE ⑨ SHT. A-11
GLAZING PUTTY
GLASS STOP BELOW
¼" STL. PL.
½" STL. PL. JAMB
HINGE
STL. DOOR
½" STL. PL. ABOVE, SEE ⑧

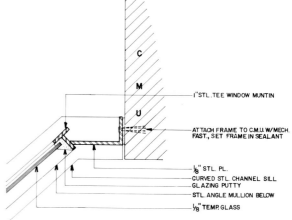

WINDOW WALL CONNECTION

C
M
U
1" STL. TEE WINDOW MUNTIN
ATTACH FRAME TO C.M.U. W/MECH. FAST., SET FRAME IN SEALANT
⅛" STL. PL.
CURVED STL. CHANNEL SILL
GLAZING PUTTY
STL. ANGLE MULLION BELOW
⅛" TEMP. GLASS

A balcony extends the axis of the addition to a view of the canyon below (above). The asymmetrical corner window acts as an inflection to distant south and west ocean views. A lightweight steel stair is inserted into one of the service towers, connecting the master suite above to the living areas below (bottom). From the master suite one looks back to the steel stair, flanked by cabinets floating above the floor (opposite).

Laguna Beach Residence

LAGUNA BEACH, CALIFORNIA

The hilltop site consists of four contiguous parcels directly overlooking the Pacific Ocean to the south and west. The strategy reorganizes the site into two distinct domains, one public and the other private. On the public side is a neighboring residence and driveway used to access the site. On the opposing side is the domain of the house, including a pool and promenade deck area, potentially an outdoor living space in the Southern California Case Study House tradition.

The parti of the intervention recognizes the dichotomy of public and private space, and provides a clear delineation of the two through the intervention of a primary wall element. Constructed of fiber cement panels, the tall wall effectively organizes the addition as closed, introverted volumes versus extroverted spaces open to the light and view of the ocean. The master bedroom is connected both literally and visually to the outdoor room of the pool by three full-height pivoting glazed doors. Acting as a tool to enhance clarity and awareness of the site, the wall is a mediator of scales, calibrating the differential between conditions on either side. The wall functions further to connect the existing house to the addition, delineating a circulation path that is illuminated by a small outdoor space formed by the two converging walls resulting from the rotation of the plan geometry.

The entry sequence, a movement from public to private zones, results in an extended threshold between volumes, contrasting the closed quality of the entry to the expansiveness of the sea beyond. After passing through a perforated metal gate and a compressed passage between the bedroom and the new poolhouse, a panoramic view of the Pacific Ocean is revealed. The act of architecture thereby amplifies the relationships between the building and nature not through mere formal emulation or invention, but instead as a tool might to establish, index, and reveal tectonic clarity, sequence, and order.

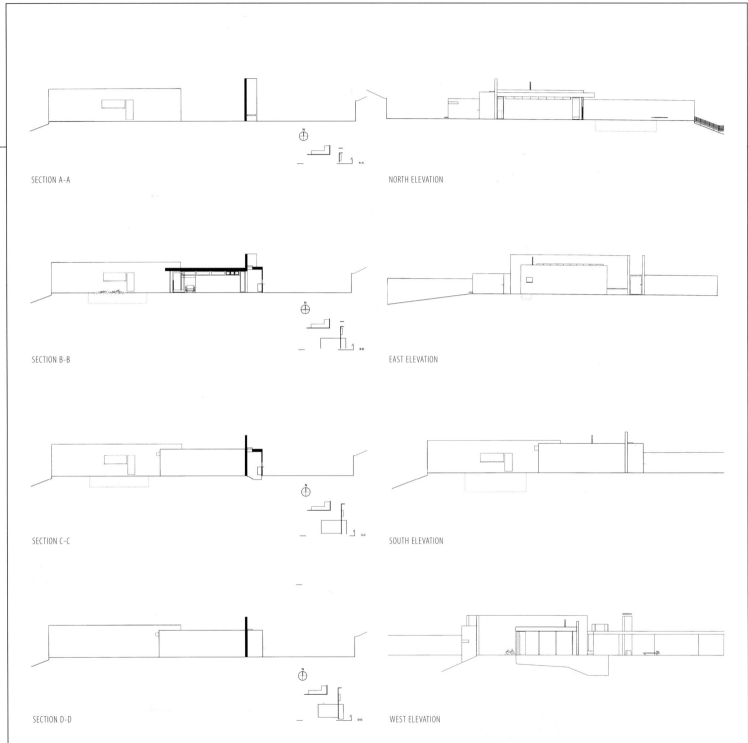

SECTION A-A

NORTH ELEVATION

SECTION B-B

EAST ELEVATION

SECTION C-C

SOUTH ELEVATION

SECTION D-D

WEST ELEVATION

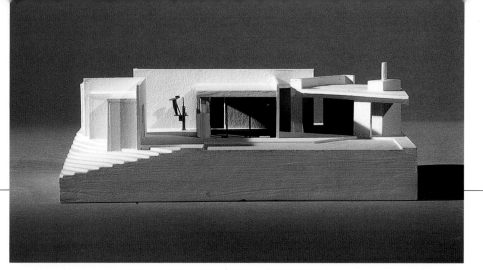

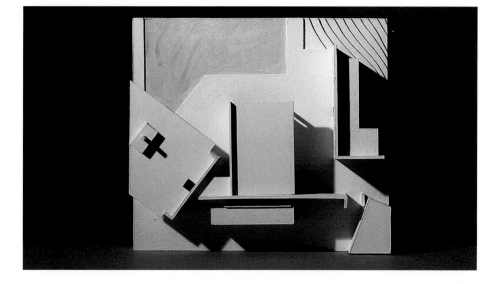

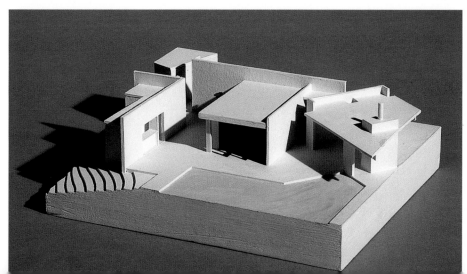

Preliminary sequential section-elevation studies (opposite). Model studies (above, center, bottom). The addition is linked to the existing house, but its autonomy clarifies and strengthens the relationships on the site between public and private spaces, views, and the new outdoor room.

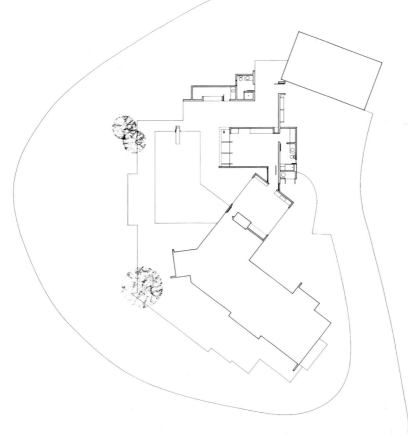

Three large custom pivoting doors (opposite) open out onto the adjacent pool, effectively connecting the bedroom to the outdoor room, and the poolhouse bar (above). The site plan shows how the entry drive spirals up and around the hill, terminating at the public side of the wall (bottom). Continuing on foot, the viewer passes into the private zone of the complex, and is compressed between building volumes, opening onto a panoramic view of the ocean horizon beyond.

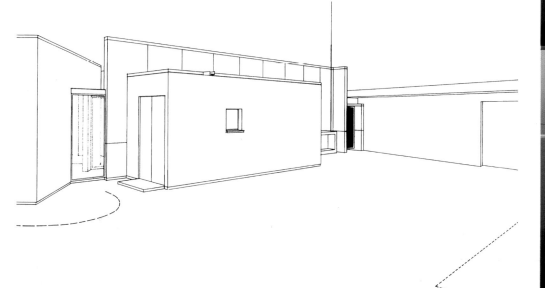

Natural light floods the guest bathroom (above). The tub and shower are inset into the floor, while black granite lavatory and wood cabinetry float above it. The interior of the master bedroom is composed of a continuous terrazzo floor with hydronic slab radiant heating, smooth trowel white plaster walls, and white oak cabinetry (opposite). Again, a simple well lit volume of space promotes the joy of living through the straightforward use of elegant, durable materials, useful and comfortable furniture, and a strong relationship to nature.

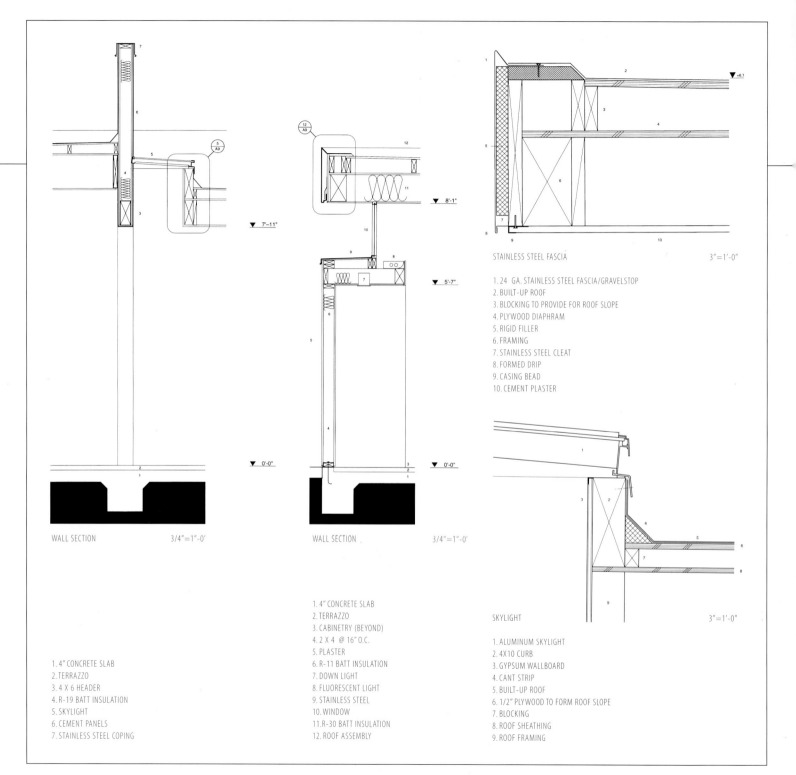

WALL SECTION   3/4"=1'-0'

1. 4" CONCRETE SLAB
2. TERRAZZO
3. 4 X 6 HEADER
4. R-19 BATT INSULATION
5. SKYLIGHT
6. CEMENT PANELS
7. STAINLESS STEEL COPING

WALL SECTION .   3/4"=1'-0'

1. 4" CONCRETE SLAB
2. TERRAZZO
3. CABINETRY (BEYOND)
4. 2 X 4 @ 16" O.C.
5. PLASTER
6. R-11 BATT INSULATION
7. DOWN LIGHT
8. FLUORESCENT LIGHT
9. STAINLESS STEEL
10. WINDOW
11. R-30 BATT INSULATION
12. ROOF ASSEMBLY

STAINLESS STEEL FASCIA   3"=1'-0"

1. 24 GA. STAINLESS STEEL FASCIA/GRAVELSTOP
2. BUILT-UP ROOF
3. BLOCKING TO PROVIDE FOR ROOF SLOPE
4. PLYWOOD DIAPHRAM
5. RIGID FILLER
6. FRAMING
7. STAINLESS STEEL CLEAT
8. FORMED DRIP
9. CASING BEAD
10. CEMENT PLASTER

SKYLIGHT   3"=1'-0"

1. ALUMINUM SKYLIGHT
2. 4X10 CURB
3. GYPSUM WALLBOARD
4. CANT STRIP
5. BUILT-UP ROOF
6. 1/2" PLYWOOD TO FORM ROOF SLOPE
7. BLOCKING
8. ROOF SHEATHING
9. ROOF FRAMING

The primary party wall separates the public space of the driveway from the private space of the outdoor room beyond (above). The wall of the pool-house bounds the northern edge of the site, and frames the view to the ocean beyond (center, bottom).

Group One Offices

When a start-up video production company decided to locate their offices in a typical California bungalow in Larchmont Village, the design problem became one of accommodating office functions while still retaining the relaxed, informal feeling of the original house. The largest room in the house, a combined living and dining room, was transformed into the reception area and conference room. Because the building owner prohibited the construction of any new walls, the challenge was to separate the two activities in the room with minimal physical change to the existing building.

The solution was to fabricate a steel and glass screen with panels that retract into the center to allow for passage. The screen floats in the room, touching the floor and ceiling at two points only, incurring minimal damage to the house while preserving the openness of the room. With this one intervention the activities are separately defined, and the translucent glass panels animate the space with the varying play of light on both sides.

Other elements of the design include an overhead lighting system and custom furniture in maple with steel and bronze details.

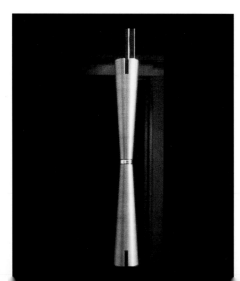

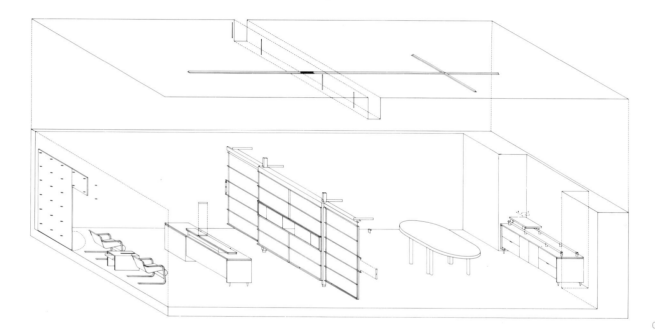

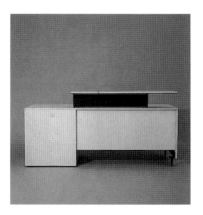

Constructed from a simple palette of materials in steel, glass, and wood, individual pieces were inserted into the existing structure to divide space and accommodate use. Furniture types were designed in response to needs that ranged from a generic desk to the more specific reception station and video monitor cabinet.

Los Angeles and the Curse of Bigness

LOS ANGELES, CALIFORNIA

The cities of our industrial age . . . have not yet found the pattern adequate to their potentialities, according to their function and technological achievement. They are paralyzed by insurmountable traffic and parking problems. They achieve no harmony in their component parts, no unity in their diversity. The discrepancy between what might be and what is grows ever wider. The very forces which made these cities grow seem to be now working toward their destruction.

Ludwig Hilberseimer, 1955

"The airplane indicts," noted Le Corbusier in 1935. The increasingly accessible view from the air suddenly revealed an urban structure never before discernible. In 1988, the view from Landsat allows us to survey still broader relationships between land masses and oceans. But at ground level, the order, hierarchy, and underlying structure perceived from above are obscured. Our point of departure is the observation that Los Angeles has been plagued by a lack of consistent direction for growth and development. A keen eye is missing. The economic exploitation of the city, along with "rampant frontierism," encourage the continual shedding of the area's morphological structure. An inspired interpretation of Los Angeles leads one to realize that a viable and complex urbanism exists. Its structure and potential, however, have been undermined by neglect, by recent decades of accelerated shifts in demographics, and by blind, insensitive growth.

The underlying structure of a city is shaped by the forces at work within the urban condition: physical (e.g. boundaries, topography), economic (land values, development), social and demographic (patterns of use and occupation). A city's legibility is fostered not by a system indiscriminately imposed over the whole, but by a latent order within each of its parts. The city as a set of individual structures, each responding to particular circumstances, forms a hierarchical whole. Contributing to a common understanding and vision, the reinforcement of underlying structure establishes a tenable principle for communication between parts. Readability of the city requires that we divine and recognize underlying structure where it exists, and impose a new structure where it does not. Not to be misconstrued as another dogmatic dictate outlining what is permissible, the concept of underlying structure is meant to feed interpretation and encourage possibility.

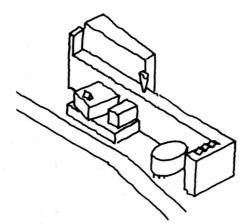

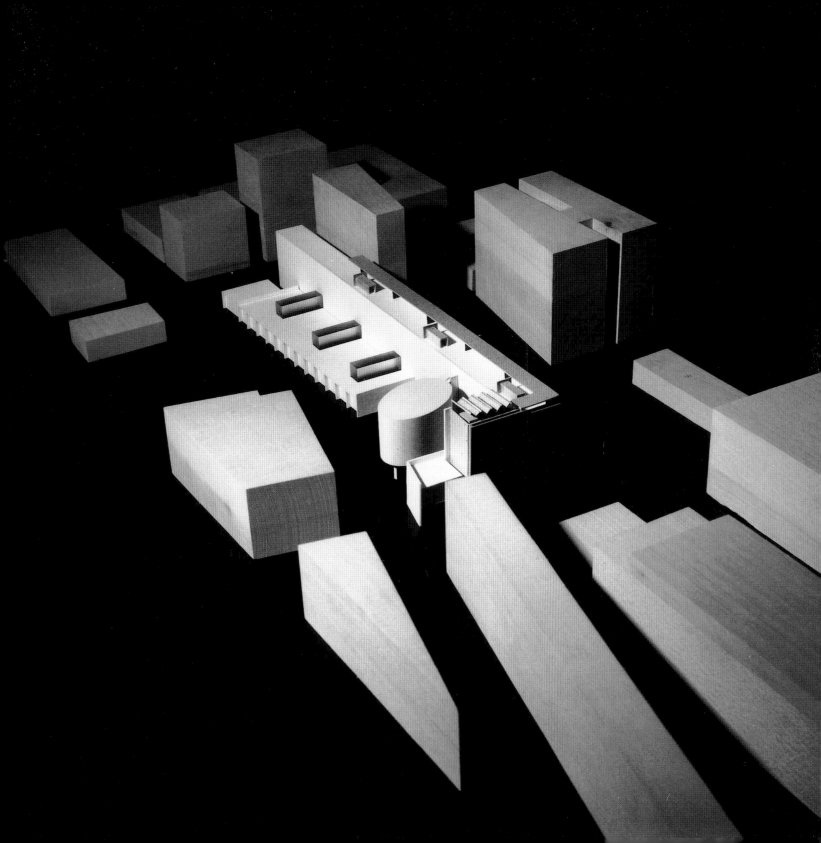

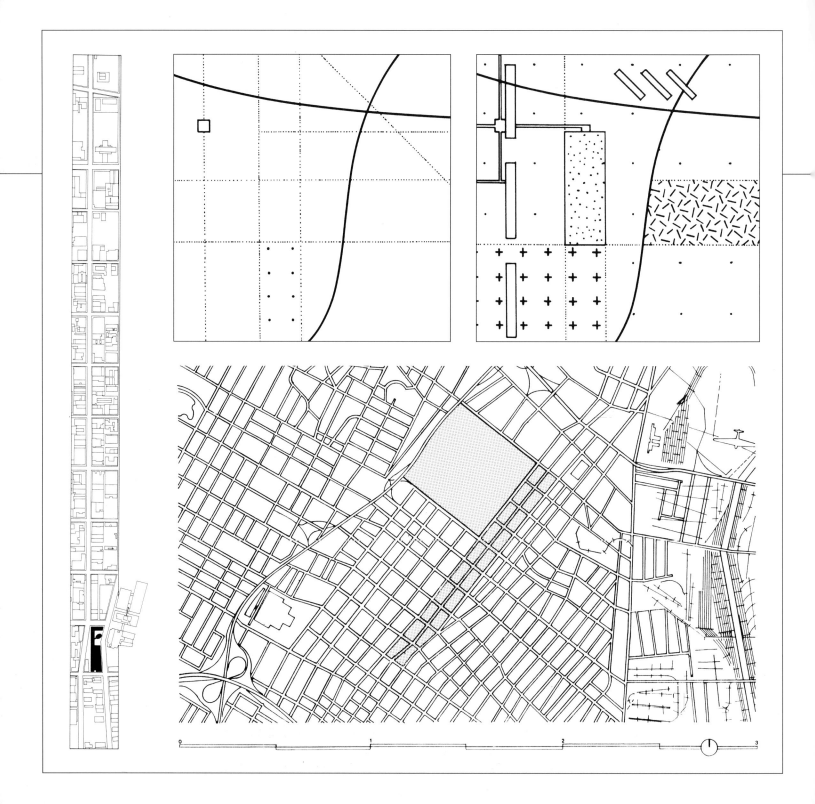

In Los Angeles order and hierarchy have become obscured. Los Angeles exists as a set of loosely related parts that have progressively lost legibility. The automobile and technology in general, backed by economic motives, have made it easier to eradicate underlying structure rather than respond to it, resulting in large areas of sameness. The existing topographical features and the transitions from one area to another are minimalized, while the whole city is covered with an infrastructure of services repeated in evenly dispersed increments. Flying above the city, the problem is evident: the same few solutions are applied indiscriminately over too large an area.

To counteract this tendency, more specific solutions are needed. Already the city strives to be a composition of parts, in municipal boundaries if not in physical form. Architecture can no longer rely upon singular conceptions of organization and planning. Planametric study must be accompanied by studies that acknowledge time, perspective, and movement as determinants of underlying structure. To increase hierarchy, we must reinforce the contrasts instead of blurring distinctions. The conception of the city must change to a series of defined, different parts expressed as areas, districts, and sub-cities that exist in relation to one another. Dynamic in their interactions, they may be equal but different, all developing in accordance with forces unique to their circumstances. A clarification of underlying structure, combined with an amalgamation of individual buildings over time, will reinforce order and readability without substituting static homogeneity. Los Angeles composed as a city of distinct parts may then begin to realize its potential, in form as well as in spirit.

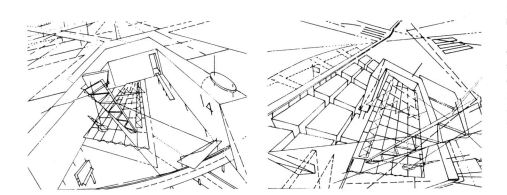

City plans indicate the locations and extent of the proposed projects (opposite). Two diagrams explain how hierarchy enhances legibility (opposite and above): the diagram on the left shows a condition of sameness, or fog, while the diagram on the right demonstrates how the insertion of a few different elements creates contrast and hierarchy, facilitating a clear reading.

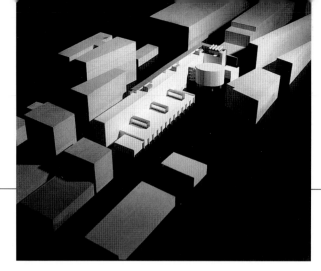

This theoretical project takes the form of two interventions in downtown Los Angeles. Each site/program/project is chosen with the intent to illustrate a clarification and reinforcement of underlying structure while maintaining its own existence and purpose as an intervention. The investigations begin to imply a critical method for action, and by extension, they exemplify tactics and principial strategies for other parts of the city.

1. The Broadway corridor is defined by a length of the street extending from the civic center to Eleventh Street in downtown Los Angeles. It is defined by buildings that follow the street edge and are usually six stories high. These buildings are serviced primarily from a system of alleys that run behind them parallel to Broadway. The underlying structure of this area is the predominance of an architecture defined along the street edge, a consistency of building height, and the distinct beginning and end of the street in its activity and use. Socially and economically it is one of the most active pedestrian streets in the city, and a place of intense commerce and social activity, with stores, restaurants, and theaters at ground level, office and living space on the floors above.

Underlying structure presents itself as the logical movement of this section of Broadway. Existing parking lots undermine the uniform street edge. Locating parking on adjacent streets will allow buildings to infill, strengthening the street edge and contributing to the continuity of street life. The proposed seven-story building, composed of living space for garment workers over commercial space at ground level, completes the street edge and acts as a transition at the bend along Broadway, marking the end of the corridor. Along Main Street, the intervention responds to the secondary condition of a loft zone within a field of blocks with smaller single-story buildings for manufacturing or showroom use. Finally, an elliptical building raised on piloti, linked by an enclosed bridge, serves as a meeting hall for the workers within the building. The form becomes a landmark or reference point, marking the shift of Main Street.

2. The second site, an area we call the Object Zone, is bounded by the Harbor Freeway to the west, Hill Street to the east, First and Fifth Streets to the north and south. The high-rise structures populating the zone make it unique in that the nature of the city block is lost. Instead, the towers and slabs become objects within a field. The underlying structure here is defined by the architectural expression of a predominant building type and a marked disintegration of the street edge, reinforced by vehicular circulation that feeds occupants into subterranean parking garages or allows them to pass through the zone via tunnels and bridges.

The new building inserted into the Broadway corridor responds to the underlying structure of a strong street edge and consistent building heights. Along Main Street, the building mass scales down to the character defined by one-story warehouse and studio spaces. The proposed building reinforces the predominant programs of the area in providing space for office and garment workers over retail at street level.

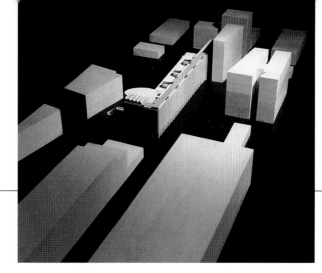

In the proposed intervention a plinth is to be constructed to create a substitute ground plane and to reinforce the nature of the zone as a random collection of objects. Above grade, pedestrian circulation and building orientation would be established free from the city grid in contrast to the system of the surrounding blocks. An area clearly defined at its perimeter and free from automobiles, the plinth would allow for the exploration of an architectural and open space that results between objects. Parks, promenades, object buildings, plazas, bridges, and viewing platforms would characterize the zone.

The plinth itself will vary in height depending upon how it meets the existing geography. The interior of the plinth will house all service functions for the buildings and spaces above, including parking. At times defined with a solid wall, at others simply as a raised platform, there will be no sidewalk at its base in order to strengthen the street as a place for the automobile and facilitate access to the support space. The plinth will engage stairways from the far edge of the encircling street and bridges crossing over to adjacent blocks and buildings. At other points it will become architectural space containing restaurants and nightclubs overlooking the city. Where the streets rise up to meet the plinth, little or no wall would exist.

Insertions that would acknowledge and enhance the context they find, these additional layers of programmatic elements would encourage coexistence and possibility. The tops of high-rise buildings would once again realize their romantic potential as destinations high above the city, for taking in the whole and feeling freedom from the surface of the earth. Didactic and provocative, the proposed intervention would extend and amend the underlying structure of the object zone, promoting a more inspired use of its position within the city.

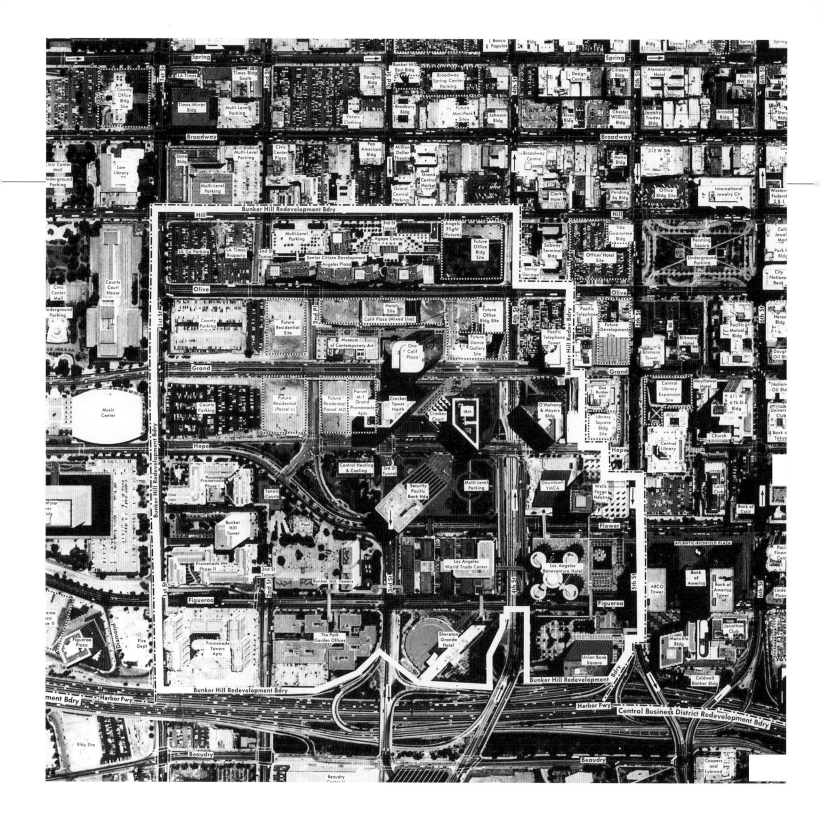

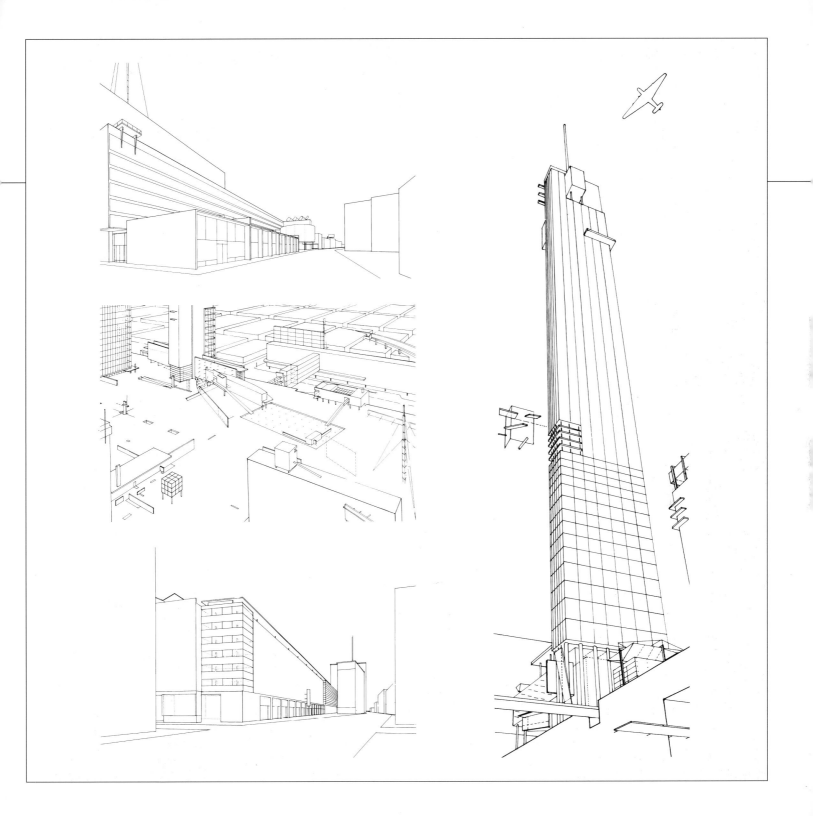

Silverlake Residence

The owner of a house asked COA to improve her kitchen and an adjacent laundry. The result was an intense analysis of the nature of these spaces in terms of dimension, equipment, and storage. Opening the kitchen to the dining and living areas and to the outdoors was given a high priority. In order to do this, no overhead cabinets were placed above the peninsula containing the cook-top or the sink area. Additionally, the small vertically proportioned window over the sink was resized to relate the counter to the space outside. To compensate for the decision not to use overhead cabinets, base cabinets were designed with deep drawers. Some of these contained shelves for the storage of dishes, garbage, recyclables, and small appliances.

The stainless-steel counters and sinks were fabricated seamlessly to provide a durable and hygienic work surface. Around the cook-top is a curved stainless-steel screen that conceals small items such as salt, pepper, and oil and is configured to precisely shield the cook-top and its activities from view. In keeping with the client's tastes, the finishes have an industrial quality not unlike a laboratory.

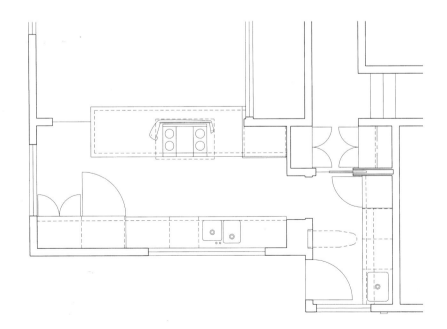

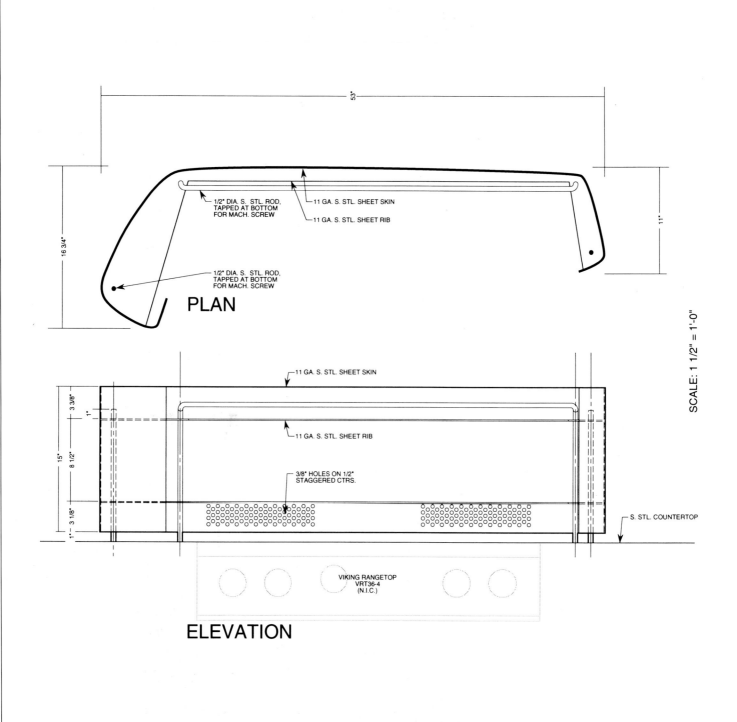

PLAN

1/2" DIA. S. STL. ROD, TAPPED AT BOTTOM FOR MACH. SCREW

11 GA. S. STL. SHEET SKIN

11 GA. S. STL. SHEET RIB

1/2" DIA. S. STL. ROD, TAPPED AT BOTTOM FOR MACH. SCREW

53"

16 3/4"

11"

SCALE: 1 1/2" = 1'-0"

11 GA. S. STL. SHEET SKIN

11 GA. S. STL. SHEET RIB

3/8" HOLES ON 1/2" STAGGERED CTRS.

S. STL. COUNTERTOP

3 3/8"
1"
15"
8 1/2"
3 1/8"
1"

VIKING RANGETOP
VRT36-4
(N.I.C.)

ELEVATION

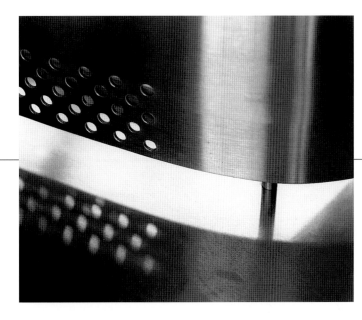

Detail of the stainless-steel cooktop screen (above). Stainless-steel countertops and plywood cabinetry make up a functional work area that mediates between the kitchen and dining spaces (bottom).

Recycling L.A.

The difference between a city and an outlying rural area is that the city has a more intense differentiation of street, building, and public space. In a city, lines of communication, transfer of goods, and movement of people are intensified and, consequently, clarity is demanded. Clarity, made possible by rules, is necessary for an understanding of the city.

These movements and exchanges occur in established patterns that both help to define and are defined by the form of the city. This urban structure is a product (result) of unwritten rules. Along with these rules, there are also exceptions. For example, in a typical American city, the through street is the rule and the dead-end street is the exception. The power of the exception is evident in the monument or government building on axis with the street, at a dead-end or T intersection. The proliferation of exceptions weakens the rule to the point of chaos.

The development of Los Angeles was from ranchos to housing tracts with scattered industries. Particular streets intensified in a grid pattern. Miracle Mile, originally developed as a retail/commercial strip midway between downtown Los Angeles and Beverly Hills, began a transformation in the fifties and sixties. The original smaller store fronts that gave a consistent presence to the area were replaced by large office complexes. Many of these office buildings were set back from the property line, perhaps to achieve an identity separate from neighboring buildings, and possibly in the hope that the space in front of these buildings would be a successful public space.

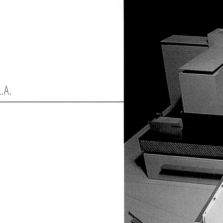

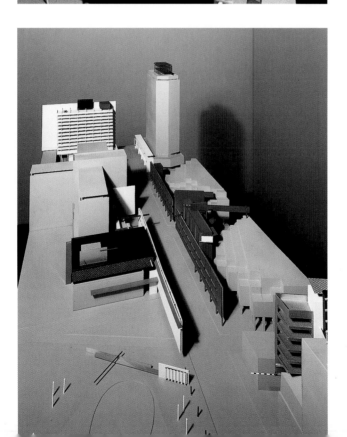

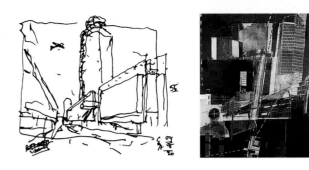

Tragically, these underused spaces have eroded the street edge, a key to understanding the city. COA's project clarifies the street, building, and public space by proposing a set of guidelines for this zone. These guidelines attempt to establish consistency by rules, both in plan and section.

GUIDELINES

Each building should consist of a mandatory base of four stories with a one-story arcade, which should maintain the property line, and an optional tower set back from the property line. In lieu of the base, a screen wall that holds the property line would be permitted.

Ground floors should be devoted to street-related businesses such as coffee bars and newsstands, while the floors above would be largely office space. Increasing contrast between the street, buildings, and public space is a step towards establishing a common architectural language in cities such as Los Angeles where none presently exists. Establishing this language is the first step if our cities are to obtain a coherent urban structure.

Wilshire Boulevard corrected: views of the model (opposite). The architectural interventions provide space for new and complementary programs while simultaneously reinforcing the linear quality of the street corridor.

Brix Restaurant

The weakening of urban space is a continual concern for COA. Piecemeal development is often detrimental to the street experience. The Brix restaurant provided COA with an opportunity to address this kind of urban degradation. Brix's location is characterized by crass commercial buildings that fail to make urban space, sited and designed without regard to each other and without relation to a concept of place. In response to this lack of coherence, COA generated a scheme that assigns functions straightforwardly and uses a filtering device to relate to the street.

The site, surrounded by one- to two-story buildings and located near a busy intersection, is constantly barraged by traffic. To counter the area's visual clutter, the design is organized as a solid kitchen box attached to a glass dining box in front. A south-facing perforated-metal screen wall, parallel to the street, serves as filtering device and links the building to the larger urban structure. In the midst of visual chaos, the screen wall presents the harried driver with a serene and comprehensible street elevation. From the building's interior it acts as shade from sun and shield from visual noise. At night the illuminated dining room projects its presence through the screen. The screen wall's perforated-aluminum skin is attached to the steel structure of an adapted advertising billboard, now a filter rather than a projection of commercial messages.

The 1,300-square-foot (117-square-meter) building consists of a large kitchen, manager's office, drive-up window, take-out counter, and small dining area. Given the limited programmatic area, the design amplifies the building's presence on the site and points to a clearer urban structure.

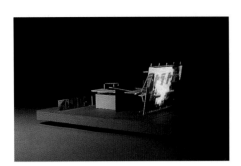

PRELIMINARY STUDIES FOR A DRIVE-THROUGH RESTAURANT

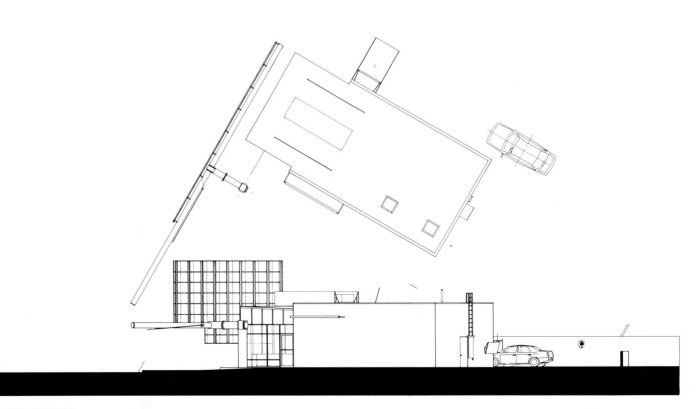

N-W ELEVATION AND ROOF PLAN

PROJECT UNDER CONSTRUCTION

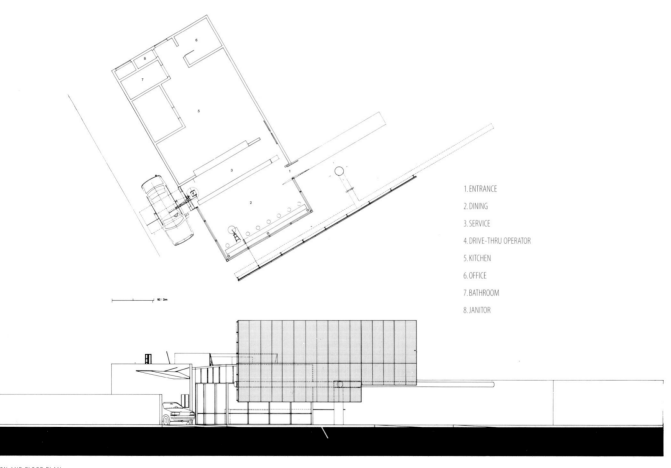

1. ENTRANCE

2. DINING

3. SERVICE

4. DRIVE-THRU OPERATOR

5. KITCHEN

6. OFFICE

7. BATHROOM

8. JANITOR

10 / 3m

S-W ELEVATION AND FLOOR PLAN

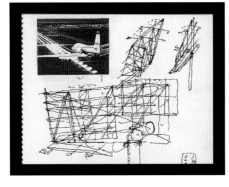

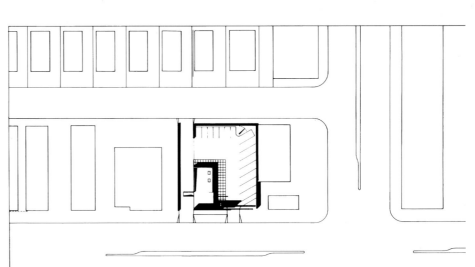

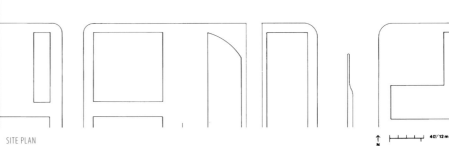

SITE PLAN

40'/12 m

N

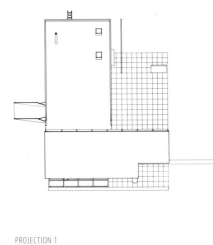

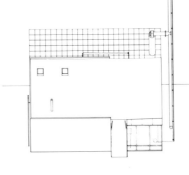

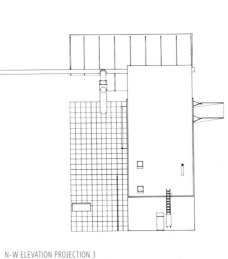

PROJECTION 1   PROJECTION 2   N-W ELEVATION PROJECTION 3

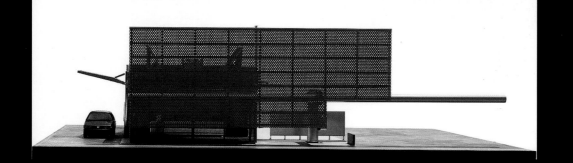

Children's play areas with morphologically designed doors: "to see the child is to protect him" (top and middle). The director's office fully glazed in order to participate completely in the life of the center (left). The whole child-care center project is organized around a unique central route whose transparency puts the garden play areas (at farthest end) in visual contact with the entrance lobby (in the foreground) (opposite page).

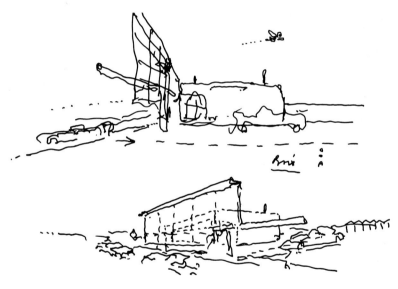

Views of the project at night show the changing character of the architecture. The luminous volume of the dining area is filtered through the screen wall, the activity within acting as a kind of urban theater.

Glendale Residence

The client's goals of art display, place for entertaining, and protected private space inspired the design of this three-bedroom house on a 16,000-square-foot (1,440-square-meter) wooded, sloping site in a residential neighborhood. The clients, two art collectors and their family, desired a clear separation between the public and private domains of the house, as well as dedicated wall space for the display of paintings and drawings.

The parti of the house separates public and private spaces of the program as two distinct volumes, connected at the main entry and organized along a series of outdoor terraces that descend with the topography of the site. The public functions to the east are placed within a single open volume as a free-plan arrangement, defined by level changes and partial-height walls. The dining room above and living room below each open out onto individual terraces to the west, but the primary view is oriented north and framed by a $12^1/_2$-foot-high (4-meter-high) window wall. Artwork is illuminated by natural, north light from the window wall, and supplemented by precisely placed skylights.

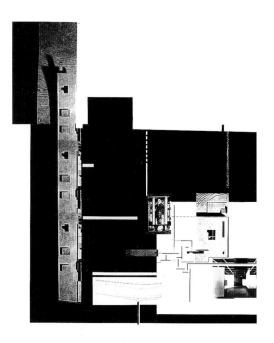

The private wing of the house is organized as an elongated rectangular bar, containing bedrooms and baths. The bar form extends into the landscape of the wooded site, effectively screening neighboring structures to the west while embracing the site interior and distant mountain views to the north. The covered master bedroom terrace remains at treetop level, floating above the land as the site drops away.

The two volumes of the house are connected at the entry, with a skylight and perforated-metal shade structure. A screen wall of the same materials encloses the entry court, mediating between the driveway and the private domain of the house.

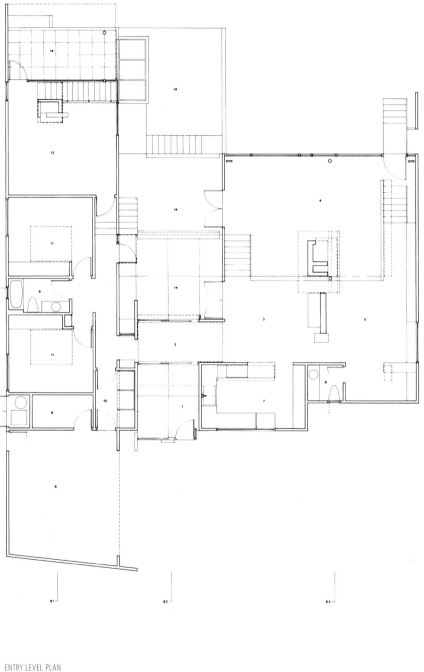

LOWER LEVEL PLAN

1. ENTRY COURT
2. ENTRY
3. DINING
4. LIVING
5. STUDY
6. BATHROOM
7. KITCHEN
8. GARAGE
9. STORAGE
10. LAUNDRY
11. BEDROOM
12. MASTER BEDROOM
13. MASTER BATHROOM
14. OUTDOOR TERRACE

ENTRY LEVEL PLAN

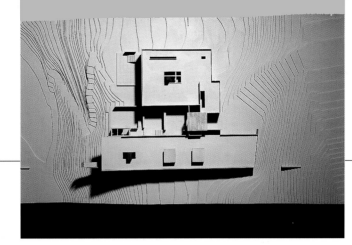

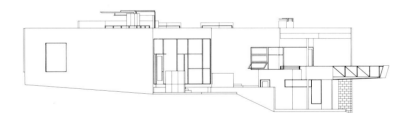

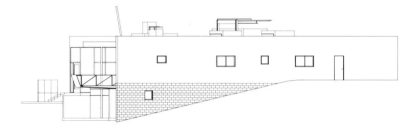

Two distinct volumes divide the public
and private domains of the house.
The bar of bedrooms extends into
nature beyond, while the living spaces
exist as a free plan defined by object-
equipment. A series of courtyards on
different levels between the volumes
respond to the natural slope of the site.

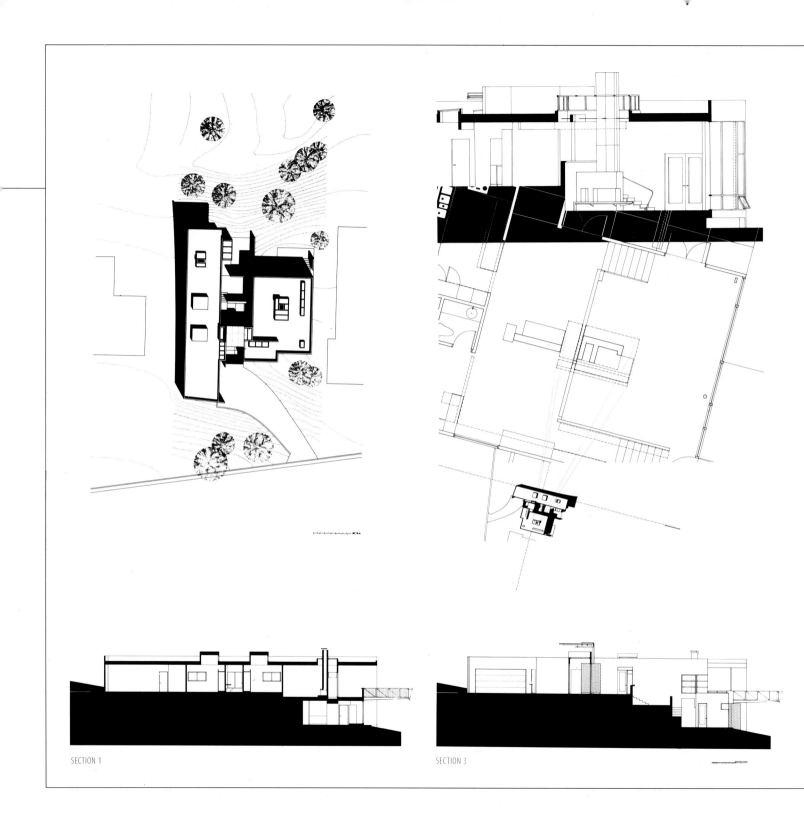

SECTION 1

SECTION 3

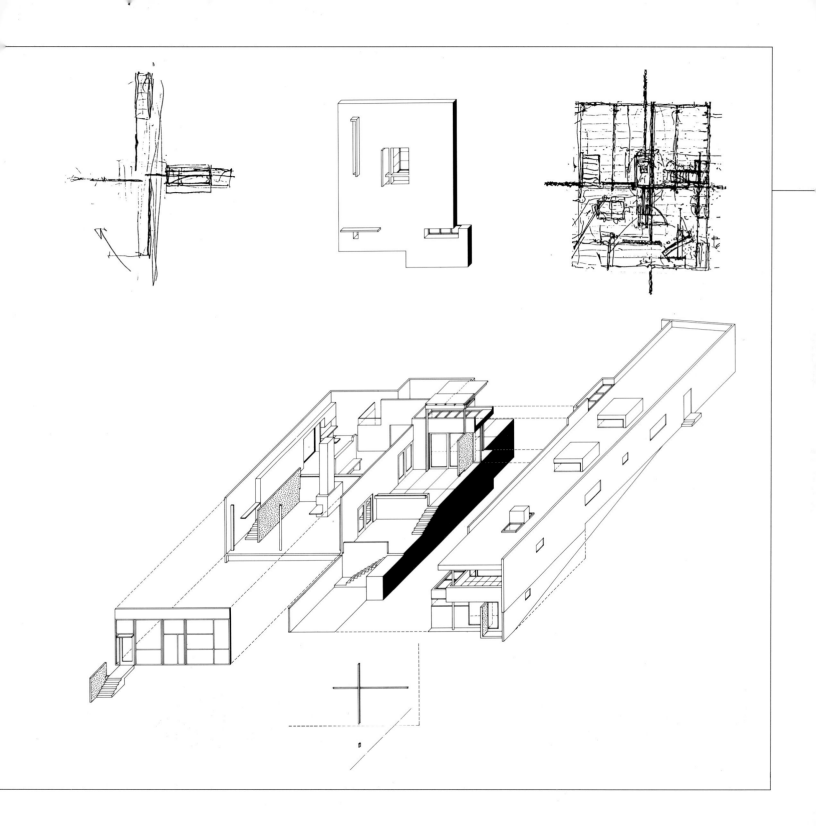

Photomontage studies of the interior spaces. The master bedroom (top) opens to the top of the oak tree canopy beyond, while the large volume of living space (center, bottom) is articulated by changes in level, building volume, and furniture.

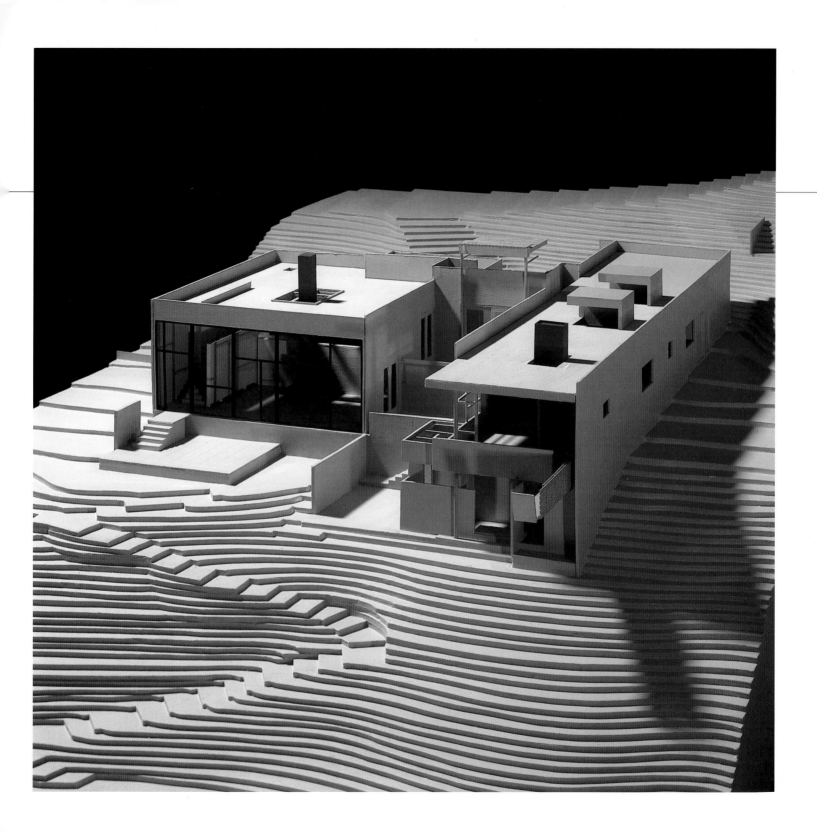

Dynamic of the Metropolis

LOS ANGELES, CALIFORNIA

Los Angeles exists simultaneously as both pre-city and post-city. Never fully becoming a city in the traditional structural sense, Los Angeles had no real perimeter separating itself from nature. Its center was at best an ambiguous set of temporary points, and certainly at the end of the twentieth century, it has far overstepped any conventional type of "contemporary city." L.A. has stretched the definition of city beyond its elastic limit. The city itself, a sprawling 467 square miles (1210 square km.), roughly equals the combined areas of St. Louis, Milwaukee, Cleveland, Minneapolis, Boston, San Francisco, and Pittsburgh. As the preeminent post-city, Los Angeles is a reduced experience, a ragged collection of distances instead of a rich mnemonic web of relationships.

COA's goal was to establish a first principle (tool) for both the analysis of Los Angeles and the production of architecture within its paradoxical locus. Apollonian clarity, order, and a legible and meaningful landscape may only be achieved and sustained by reinforcing underlying structure.

The investigation site is an area 3300 feet x 5280 feet (1000 meters x 1620 meters) located in downtown Los Angeles. The site stands out because of its inherently complex and layered condition, characterized by COA as a collision of an incomplete set of structures and corresponding substructures. On this found condition, the investigation is performed through an overlay of ideas and a series of multi-scaled operations yielding a didactic map.

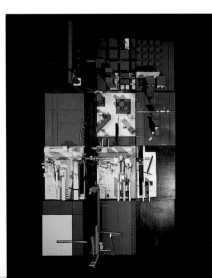

The site can be analyzed as a Venn diagram containing an intersection of various urban structures. The Harbor freeway acts as a linear slot dividing the Bunker Hill redevelopment from the northwest sector of downtown; the city of blocks to the south contrasts with the free distribution of medium- and high-rise office towers in the object zone. The site is a repository of information (i.e., built form) over time, rendered as both overlay and erasure of underlying structure(s).

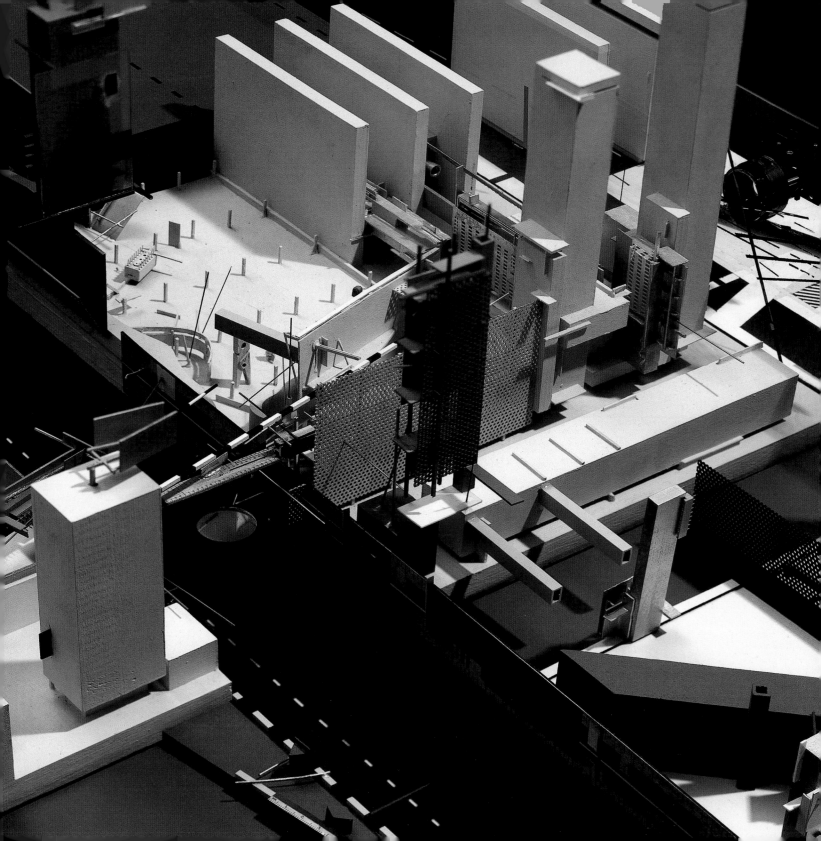

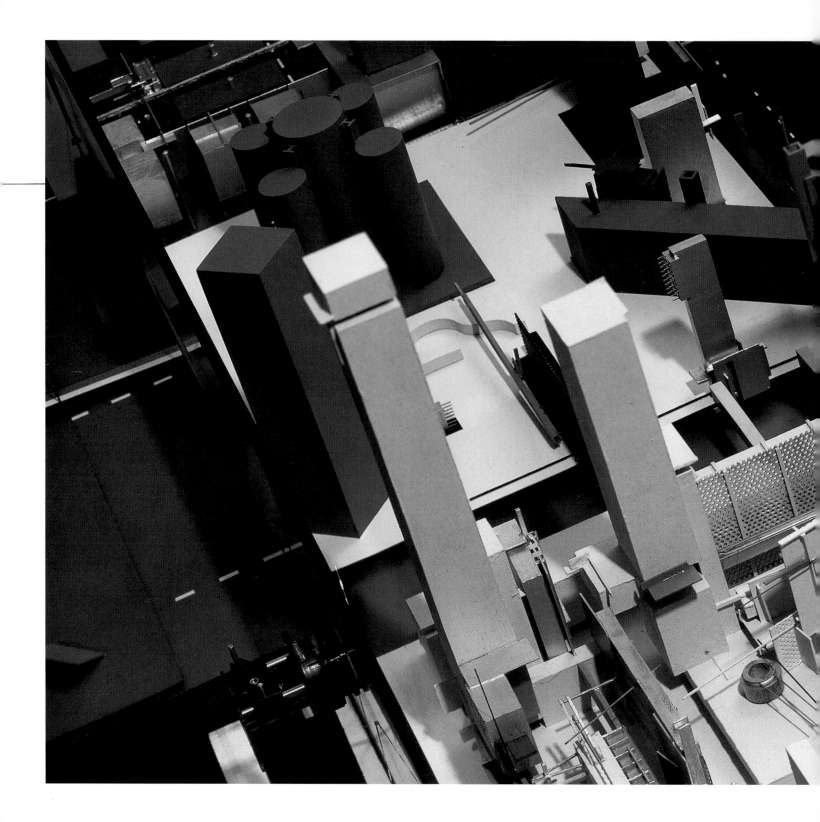

Restroom Prototype

The design of this prototype addresses the primary problems of the typical park restroom facility: a lack of sufficient lighting, inadequate ventilation, excessive maintenance, and the safety of the user. Inspiration for the design came from the ubiquitous industrial infrastructural fragments found in Southern California. Without being overly self-conscious, these pieces of infrastructure silently perform their jobs. COA adapted these materials and construction methods to design the 630-square-foot (57-square-meter) restroom and storage space.

In order to correct for inadequate lighting, the prefabricated roof trusses of the prototype are covered with translucent polycarbonate, diffusing natural light into the facility below. Exterior supplementary lights are used when necessary and at night, lights within illuminate the roof as a visible landmark that adds to the visual landscape. Ample ventilation is achieved by separating the roof from the lower concrete structure. Restrooms of different capacities are accommodated simply by varying the length of the project.

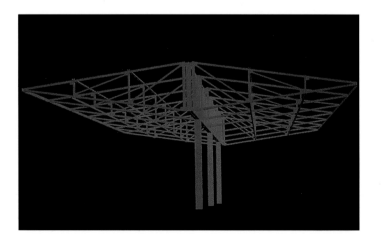

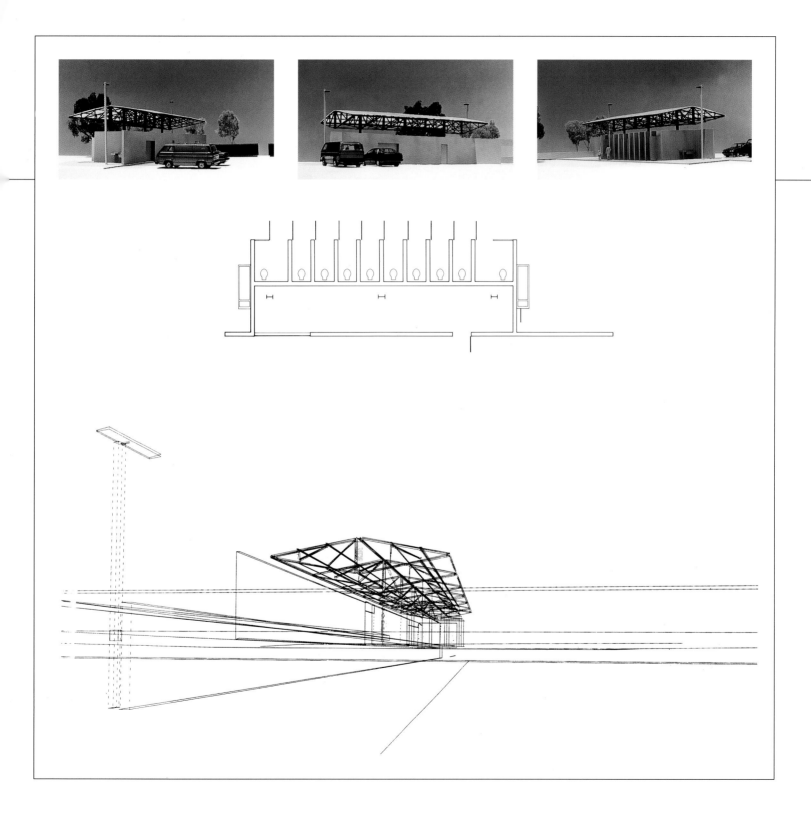

Hawkes Studio

LOS ANGELES, CALIFORNIA

Given the problem of expanding a photographer's studio in an existing one-story industrial building, the best alternative was to expand vertically. The program called for the addition of a new rooftop apartment, outdoor shooting studio, and garage. The site was a 7,200-square-foot (648-square-meter) parallelogram in midtown Los Angeles, located at the corner of a primary boulevard and side street.

The apartment is proposed as an autonomous building floating above the rooftop of the existing structure, adjacent to a large outdoor shooting studio composed of perforated-steel deck over a moment-resistant steel frame. The steel frame hovers approximately six feet (two meters) above the existing roof and is supported on six steel columns that strategically penetrate the building below. Conceived as a building over a building, the parti minimizes the impact of the intervention on the existing building, allowing the new ground-plane to remain autonomous from and coexistent with the existing roofscape. A series of extruded skylights march rhythmically through the existing roof and new studio terrace above. The solution proposes a new garage with secured entry and storage area as an addition on the ground floor at the rear of the building. As a bar element of equal height to the existing building, it screens the ground-level outdoor area from the adjacent street and alley, and defines the perimeter of the site. Its roof is used as an outdoor terrace and additional shooting area.

Finally, the photographer's office, located in the existing structure, has a small private room above, suspended within the last skylight. Located in the ceiling of this introverted space is a camera obscura, projecting views of the surroundings onto a table-top surface when the space is darkened. The camera obscura functions as an architectural element/machine that re-establishes connection to the city and the landscape, projecting beyond the immediate context to imply larger-scale relationships.

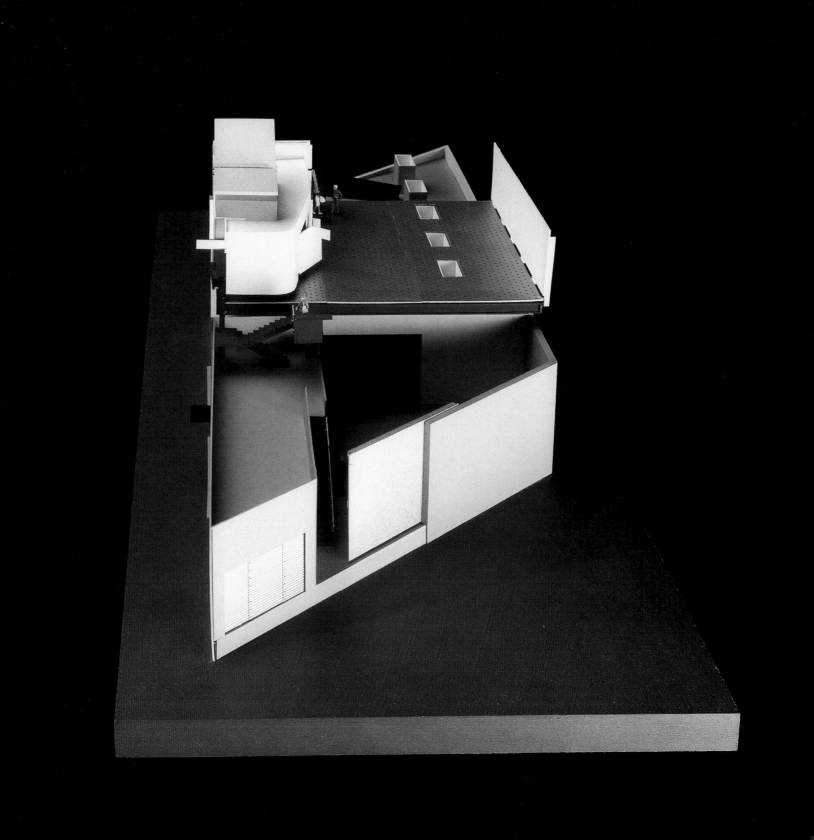

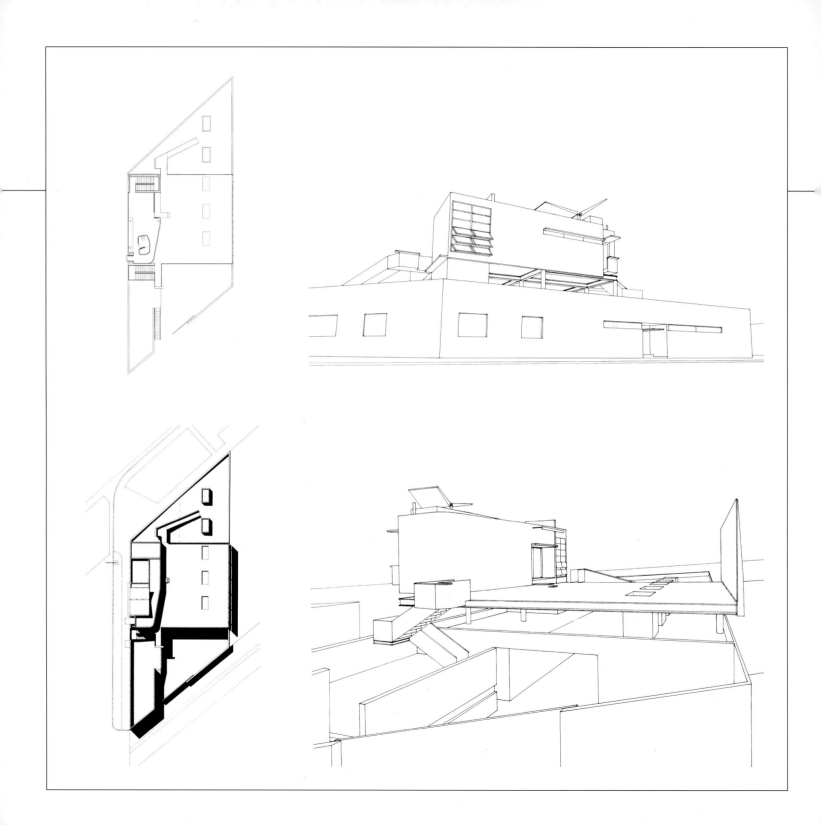

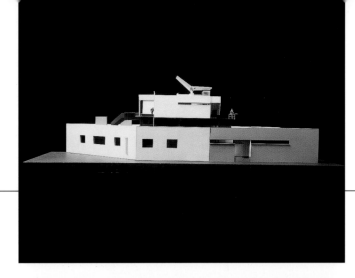

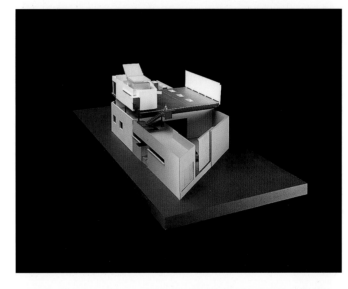

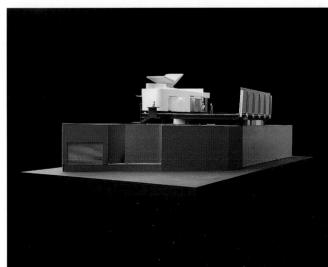

The apartment hovers above the existing warehouse structure, surrounded by a new ground plane that acts as an outdoor studio area.

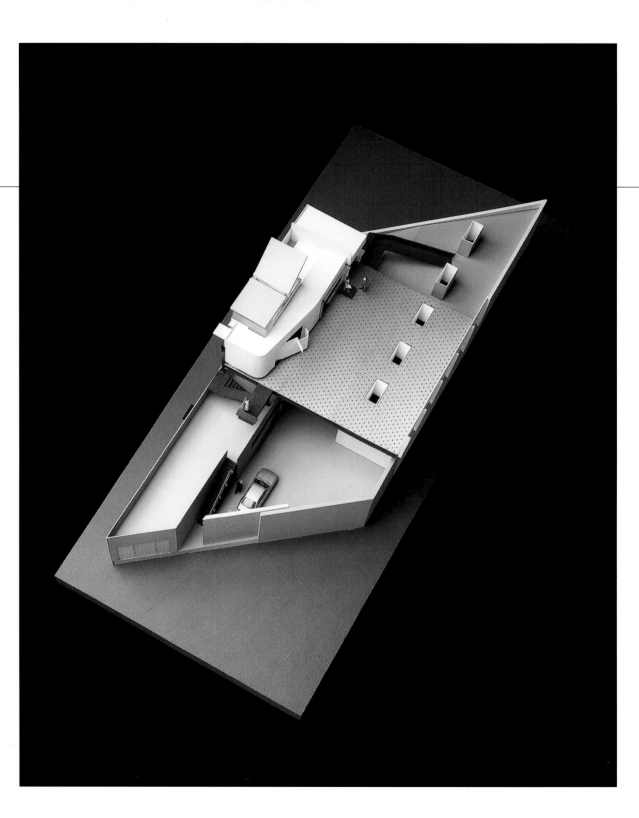

The enclosure of the parallelogram-shaped site is completed by the addition of a new garage and entry area along the eastern perimeter. The roof of this new building provides additional studio area and acts as an intermediate zone between the primary and the new grounds.

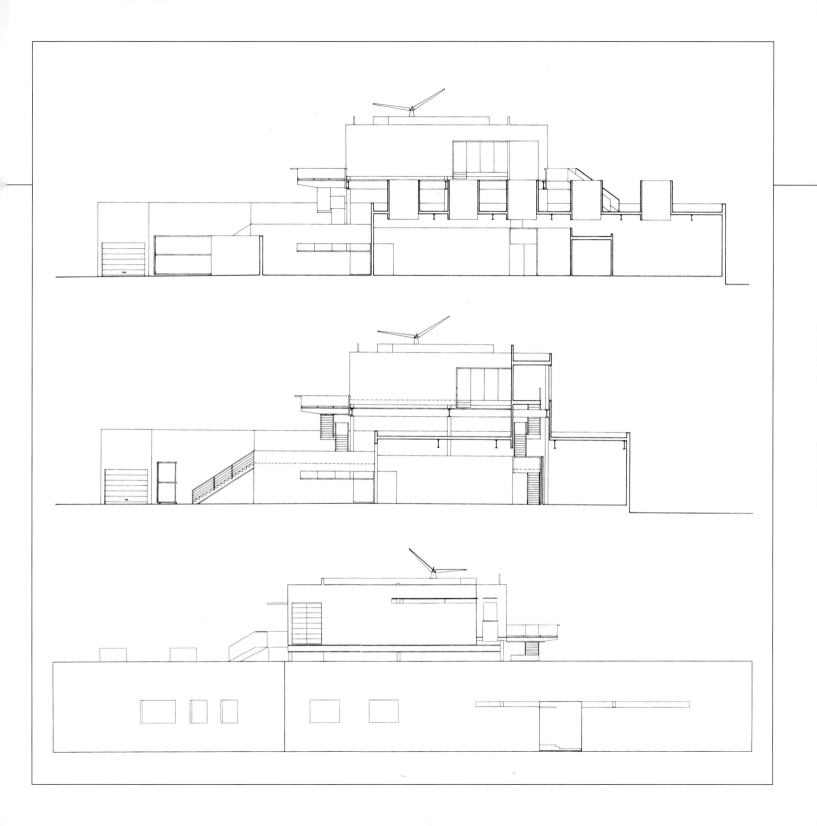

Re: American Dream

Los Angeles, it should be understood, is not a mere city. On the contrary, it is, and has been since 1888, a commodity; something to be advertised and sold to the people of the United States like automobiles, cigarettes, and mouth wash.[1]

Los Angeles has seen unprecedented and rampant exploitation by hegemonic political and economic forces that dissolve the public realm of the city into a seamless horizontal experience of bankrupt formal gestures devoid of value either urbanistically or architecturally. Greed, in the form of the capitalist machine, combined with "rampant frontierism",[2] have left the city in the hands of extraordinary rapists who control and continuously exploit the city toward solely speculative (financial, political) ends. This violence has left in its wake slums and decaying neighborhoods, victims of the continuous interruption and erasure of hierarchy as the measure of a legible and sentient experience within the urban grid. Nostalgia for the myth of its own fictitious past creates a pervasive and amplified dementia that vividly portrays the misery and blasé[3] of the contemporary urban experience. Lacking an awareness of its own essence,[4] Los Angeles lies directionless, forever folding in on itself, a pathetic homogeneity.

Morphologically, Los Angeles is a complex hybrid; its unstable and shifting form exists in a flux somewhere between the traditional European city model of fabric and corridor streets, and the modernist conception of the city as object-buildings in the park. The traditional city is primarily an experience of spaces defined by continuous walls of building, arranged in a way that emphasizes the figure of the void and de-emphasizes the building volumes. The modernist conception, espoused by Le Corbusier, is phenomenally an opposite model: it is one of discrete three-dimensional objects floating in space,

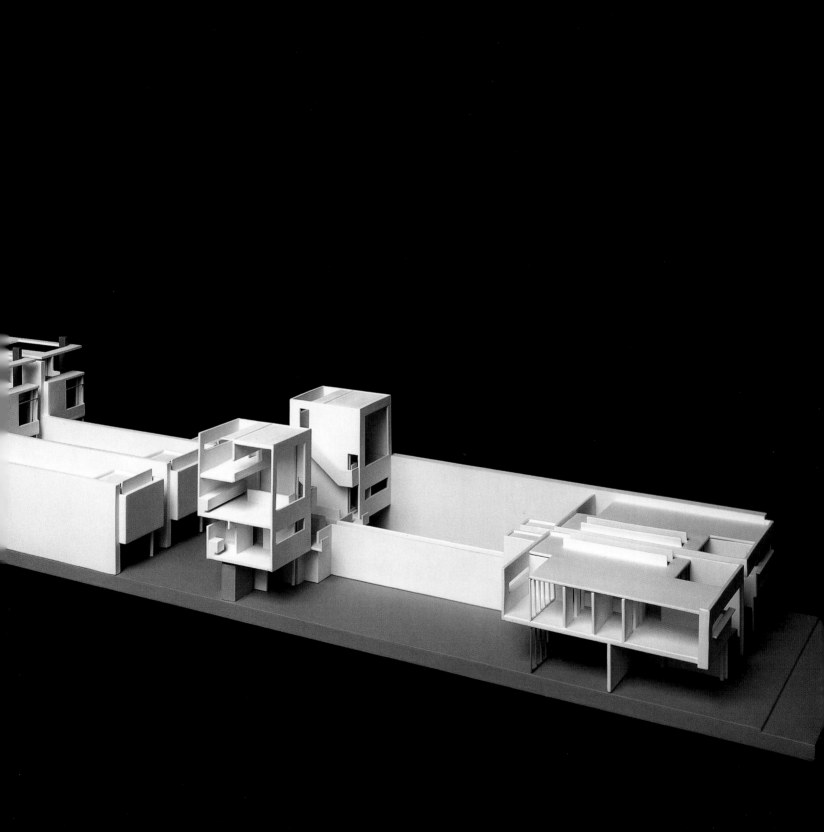

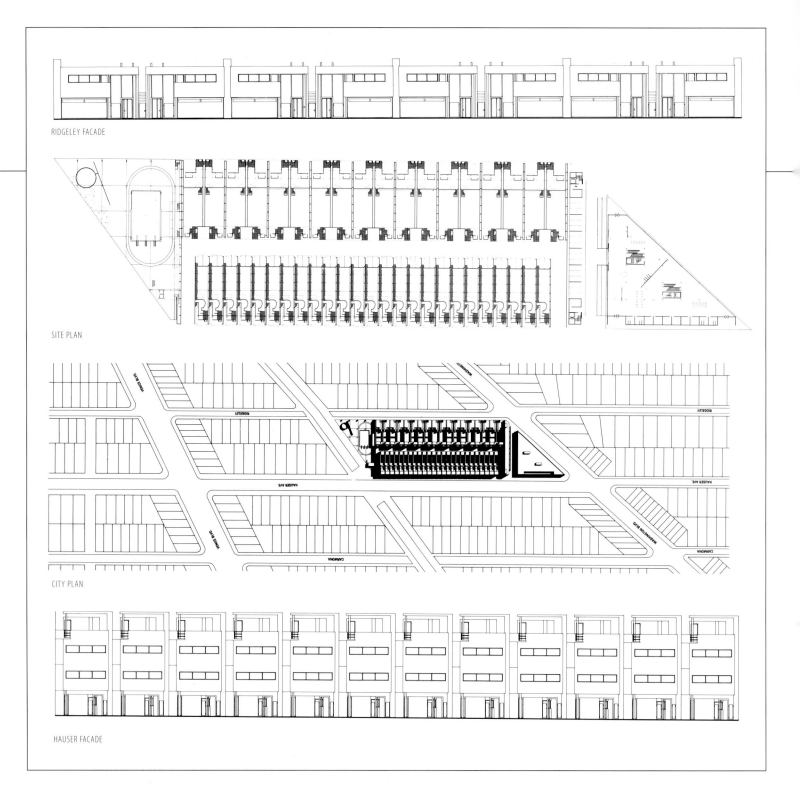

RIDGELEY FACADE

SITE PLAN

CITY PLAN

HAUSER FACADE

amplifying their autonomy and individuality while defying gravity. Los Angeles, existing in a zone that simultaneously suggests and denies either or both of these models, posits perhaps a third alternative, that of the post-city. The condition of the post-city is characterized by the coexistence of contradictory and incompatible elements, causing an irresolvable aporia. The post-city, unable to construct and differentiate relationships, attenuates experience through an infinitely expanding and accelerating web of non-hierarchical traced paths. The previous definitions of city are superseded; the possibility of a totalizing portrait is eliminated, rendered inconceivable and inappropriate.

> It is impossible to say precisely when one can begin to speak of the existence of two distinct and bitterly conflicting modernities. What is certain is that at some point during the first half of the nineteenth century an irreversible split occurred between modernity as a stage in the history of Western civilization—a product of scientific and technological progress, of the industrial revolution, of the sweeping economic and social changes brought about by capitalism—and modernity as an aesthetic concept.[5]

Here Matei Calinescu describes a conception of modernity polarized by the irreconcilable opposition between the sets of values corresponding to (1) the objectified, socially measurable time of capitalist civilization (time as a more or less precious commodity, bought and sold on the market), and (2) the personal, subjective, imaginative *durée*, the private time created by the unfolding of the "self." The latter identity of time and self constitutes the foundation of modernist culture. The current pluralist condition of the postmodern has left Los Angeles in the unstable state of an urban palimpsest, a metropolitan text undergoing erasure and layering in such a way as to become the equivalent of a multiple-exposure photograph: ambiguous and open for multiple readings at best, entropic noise at worst. A post-existentialist value system confuses the loss of the first principle, the reliable and definitive reference point (and for better or worse, a source of the collective will) with that of a solipsistic narcissism, symptomatic of a pathology brought on by the forces of late-capitalism. The result is a vacuous condition that resists coherence and falsely relieves the citizen of responsibility to any larger, collective conception of the metropolis. Radical privatization, the ideology of consumption, fear of boredom, and the need for escape leave contemporary metropolitan Los Angeles with a misconception of freedom as pluralism and chaos.[6]

The instabilities of the modern metropolis are juxtaposed and played for their theatricality in Jacques Tati's film, *Mon Oncle* (1956). Monsieur Hulot lives in a penthouse above a typically quaint French place, where he has daily encounters with his neighbors. Hulot enjoys rotating his bedroom window in order to reflect sunlight into a neighbor's window, blinding a noisy pet parrot. Situated in both a morphologically and demographically stable part of the city, Monsieur Hulot's relationship to the city is one

This project for urban housing addresses the area of a typical inner-city block (opposite). While the end conditions are anchored by a large commercial building along Venice Boulevard and a public park/greenbelt along the river, the body of the site is populated by the different housing types.

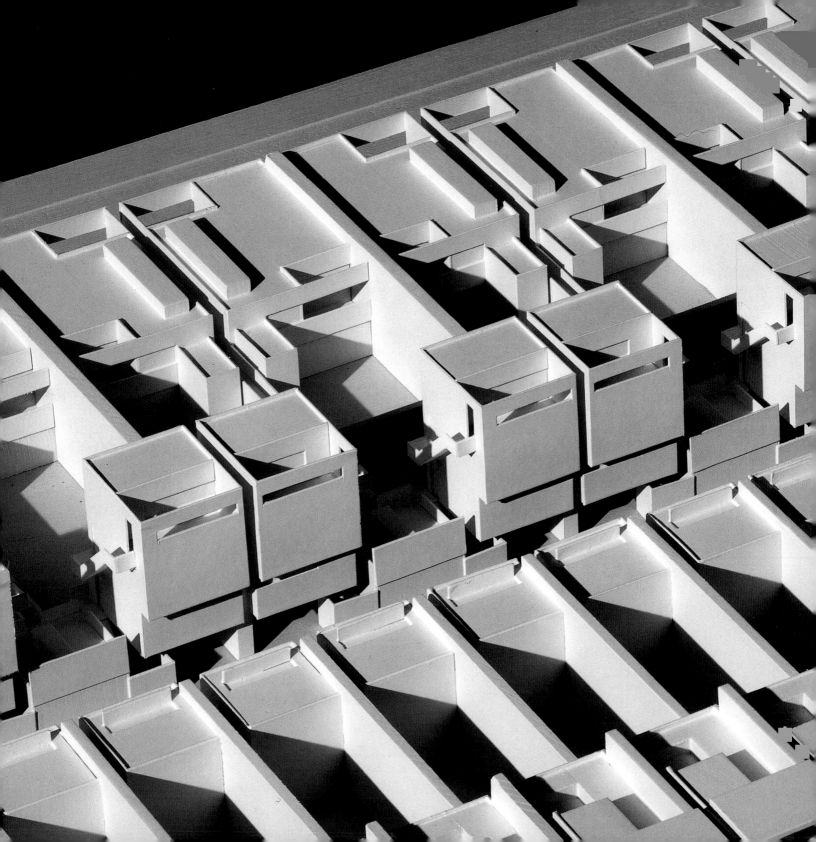

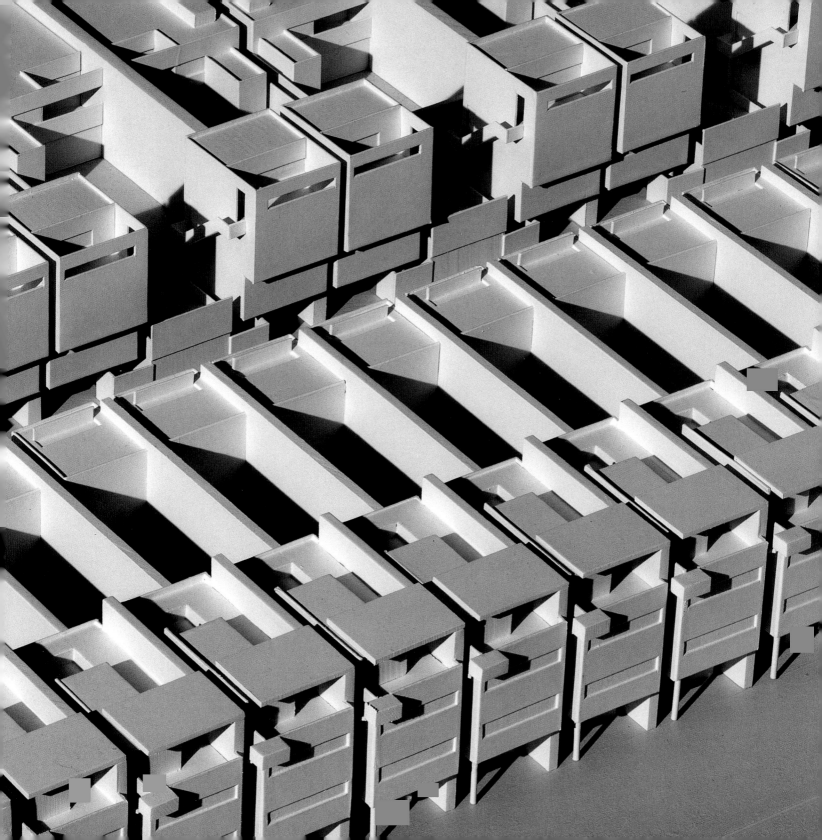

of exterior openness and interaction. At the same time, in another part of the city, Hulot's well-off sister lives within a walled modernist compound where life becomes one of separation and repose, where the city itself is effectively shut out. Everyday experience is radically internalized, resulting in an amplified response to its contained site.

Our assumption is that one cannot play both sides in this scenario; housing in the city cannot simultaneously contain both of these conditions without contradiction. Radical privatization[7] on both the corporate and individual level has all but ended the need and desire for public space in metropolitan Los Angeles. Actual space in the unstable capitalist metropolis,[8] displaced by technological advancement and consequent alterations in sociocultural phenomena, has been replaced with collapsed space.[9] The circumspect form of simulated space and communication networks exemplify the rapidity of transformation, organization, and simultaneity of communications, as well as the city's accelerated tempo of use, eclecticism, and technological fetishism.[10] These side effects of modernity, if not problematized, reduce the artistic experience of architecture to a pure object (an obvious metaphor for object-merchandise), where the criterion of economic obsolescence overrides all others.

Faced with the reality that orgies of construction during economic booms have made a mess of our urban life, it seems imperative to stop and reflect critically on the project itself, to open a window of optimism amidst the neglect and disinvestment that has plagued entire urban sectors. The critical architectural response must be one of opposition to Los Angeles's indiscriminate growth. While accepting the inherent contradictions of time and place, it must respond to them in a manner that adds hierarchy and hence legibility to the experience of the city.

Each housing unit opens onto a private outdoor courtyard space, reinforcing a common Southern California typology. The section through the block (bottom) shows the different scales of housing types, each in response to their surroundings. The organization of the block is defined by infrastructural service walls that provide and route all utilities.

This work stands as a substantive contribution toward the establishment of a praxis regarding architectural interventions[11] within the grid of Los Angeles. It does not argue for the final form of the city, but instead posits a critical reading of the situation based on certain criteria. Judgments can then be made and directed toward a meaningful architectural intervention. The work is a hypothesis about the ordering of events, countering hegemonic political, social, and economic tendencies, and proposes with fixed and measured results a tenable model of future proposals for housing fabric within the city. Under such circumstances, what is needed is not the naïve and nostalgic simulation of "the front porch" but instead "housing" as a proposition that reveals its own true presence based on values that critique the existing paradigm of both the structure of the individual dwelling and the morphology of the city. The formal and conceptual continuity of the intervention transcends its functionalist origin and becomes part of the memory of the city itself as it is traversed by both time and experience. The totalization of the block reinforces its ability to resist the shifting of hegemonic forces that surround it. As an unexecuted project, the proposal seeks to free itself from specific zoning restrictions, the

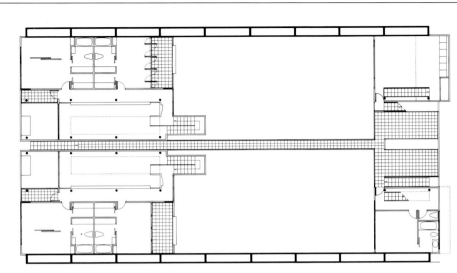

FIRST FLOOR PLANS

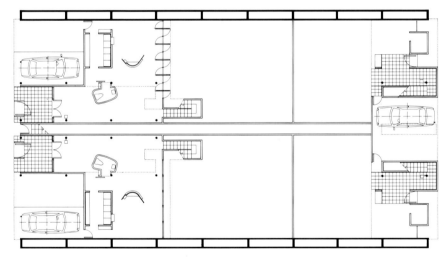

GROUND FLOOR PLANS

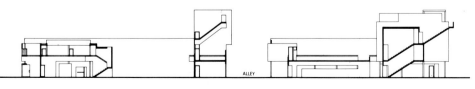

SECTION   ALLEY

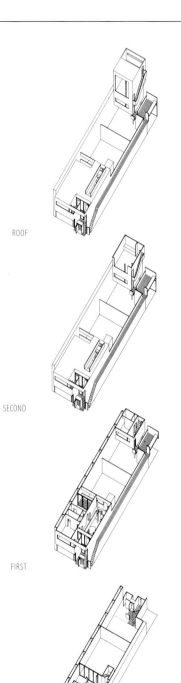

ROOF

SECOND

FIRST

GROUND

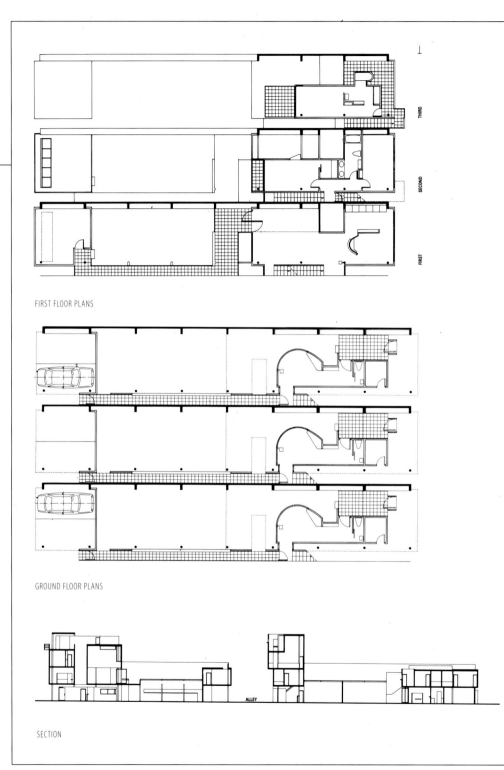

FIRST FLOOR PLANS

GROUND FLOOR PLANS

SECTION   ALLEY   RIDGELEY

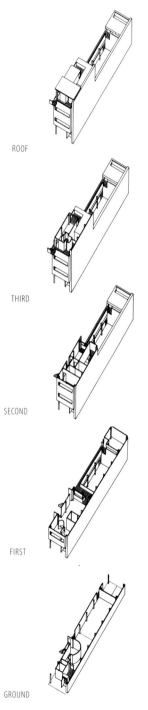

ROOF

THIRD

SECOND

FIRST

GROUND

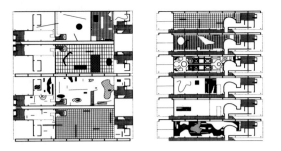

residue of archaic codes, in order to show that with sober thinking and analysis, the problem of housing can be resolved in architectural form. Its representative form is meant to embody a coherent expression of our beliefs regarding the status of the role of architects working within a critical framework.

The unfolding evolution of the city cell or dwelling can be seen as the history of evolving a model for habitation. Le Corbusier's proclamation, "The house is a machine for living in"[12] demanded a paradigm shift away from what he clearly viewed as an outdated and wholly inhumane condition of life for modern humanity. It is a misreading to understand Le Corbusier's proclamation as supportive of the machine aesthetic. It was clearly a demand for culture to come to grips with the logic and perfection of "a problem clearly stated," and the necessity of architecture and lifestyle to reconcile themselves with technology. The white villas, then, must be critiqued in relation to the active adaptation of the individual to technological reality and the new spatial conditions that such a reality imposes. Our intention is to reinvest space in the condition of modernity, space that has been occluded by the polarity Calinescu described. In order to escape the commodification of the "house" as a fetishistic autonomous object, exemplified by the Case Study House program in Los Angeles in the late 1950s, we choose to focus on the morphology of the block and the house type as integral parts of the city's fabric.[13] We believe in the tangible and clear achievement of the modernist project recontextualized, which leads to the conviction that it is far from bankrupt in its various contemporary manifestations, and that through our own comment we have progressed far from its Eurocentric origin.

The idea of "context" is seen conceptually as an equation where the value of the existing block structure is weighed against the value of the proposed intervention. The intervention is a critical discourse on urban housing and its relation to the city; it embraces the grid[14] as a basic organizational language in order to manifest a legible diagram in contrast to the intolerable situation that surrounds it.

DENSIFY OR DIE

The need to densify housing will bring about certain changes. Open space in residential quarters must be devoted either to streets or to real human activity instead of useless side and front yards. In order to achieve more density, buildings must have smaller footprints and consequently push upwards.

The increase in density will require a shift from the current definition of suburban space by trees, shrubs, and low fences to an urban definition of space by buildings, courts, and high walls. While increases in density will result in decreased use of the car, the car and house will remain inextricably linked.

Courtyard scripts: permutations of the American dream (above). The courtyard becomes a potential site for the projection of the individual's need and desire for the manifestation of myth and ritual.

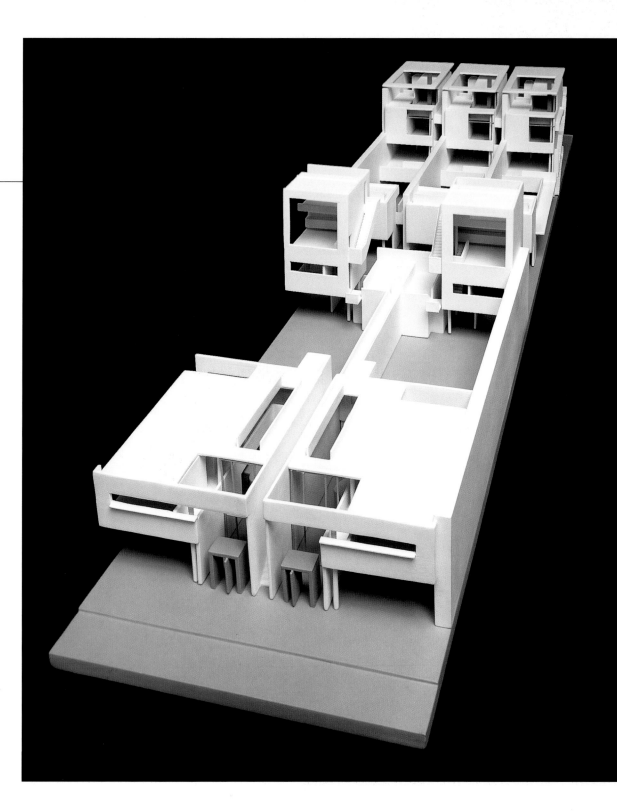

Exhibition installation (opposite, top left). Hauser unit study model (bottom left). Hauser Boulevard facade (right). The three unit types, as seen from Ridgely Avenue (this page).

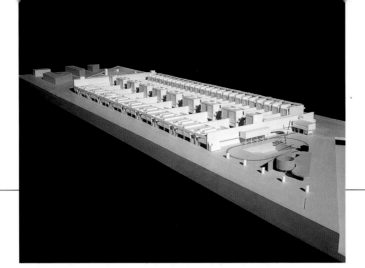

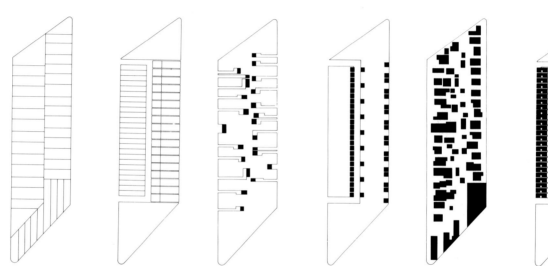

The diagrams demonstrate the advantages of the new typologies as they relate to property divisions, access, and usable outdoor space (center right). Sketches describe some of the spaces within each of the units (opposite). The party walls provide privacy and shade, and define the outdoor courtyards.

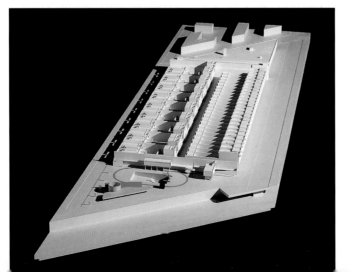

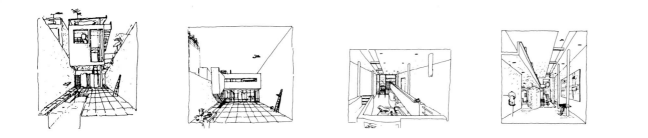

The form of the American Dream embodied in the single-family detached suburban house is irreconcilable with the inevitable increase in population density and the potential for a quality urban experience. A new type of urban house must develop which retains the most important aspects of the American Dream: individual home and land ownership and the preservation of private space.

NOTES

1. Morrow Mayo, Los Angeles(New York, 1993).Quoted in Mike Davis, *City of Quartz: Excavating the Future in Los Angeles* (New York, 1990): 319.

2. Central Office of Architecture, "Los Angeles and the Curse of Bigness," in *Offramp* (1989).

3. "The essence of the blasé attitude (towards the city) consists of the blunting of discrimination. This does not mean that the objects are not perceived, as in the case with the half-wit, but rather, that the meaning and differing values of things, and thereby the things themselves, are experienced as insubstantial. They appear to the blasé person in an evenly flat and gray tone; no one object deserves preference over any other. This mood is the faithful subjective reflection of a completely internalized money economy . . . all things float with equal specific gravity in the constantly moving stream of money. All things lie on the same level and differ from one another only in the size of the area which they cover." Georg Simmel, "Die Grossstadt und das Geistesleben" (Dresden, 1903). Eng. trans., "The Metropolis and Mental Life" in *The Sociology of Georg Simmel*, trans. and ed. Kurt H. Wolff (New York, 1950): 409–24.

4. See Heidegger's lecture, "The Question Concerning Technology." His definition of "essence" shows that it does not simply mean what something is, but that it means further the way in which something pursues it course, the way in which it remains through time as what it is. It also must be understood as "presencing" or "coming to presence", which gives the word a contextual reference to time and becoming. Heidegger states: "Modern technology too is a means to an end. That is why the instrumental conception of technology conditions every attempt to bring man into the right relation to technology. Everything depends on our manipulating technology in the proper manner as a means. We will master it. The will to mastery becomes all the more urgent the more technology threatens to slip from human control."

5. Matei Calinescù, *Five Faces Of Modernity* (Durham, North Carolina 1987): 5.

6. Tafuri, in discussing the state of the twentieth-century capitalist metropolis states, "Of course, chaos is a datum and order an objective; it is sought within it. It is order that confers significance upon chaos and transforms it into value, into 'Liberty'." Manfredo Tafuri, *Architecture and Utopia: Design and Capitalist Development* (Cambridge, Massachusetts, 1976): 96.

7. Fifty percent of telephone numbers in California are unlisted (Pacific Bell 1991).

8. "Capitalist development must negotiate a knife edge between preserving the values of past commitments made at a particular point in time, or devaluing them to open up fresh room for accumulation. Capitalism perpetually strives, therefore, to create a social and physical landscape in its own image and requisite to its own needs at a particular point in time, only just as certainly to undermine, disrupt and even destroy that landscape at a later point in time. The inner contradictions of capitalism are expressed in the restless formation and reformation of geographical landscapes. This is the tune to which the historical geography of capitalism must dance without cease." Harvey (1985): 150. See Edward W. Soja, *Postmodern Geographies: The Reassertion of Space in Critical Social Theory* (New York, 1989): 157.

9. "The superimposed layers of the recombinant image share the similar 'thinness' of Duchamp's infrathin. These layers exist in a collapsed (discontinuous) space time, that unstable plane where disparate elements are forced to coexist. Phenomenally, this collapse results in the compression of experience." Central Office of Architecture, *Recombinant Images in Los Angeles* (Los Angeles, 1989).

10. Jean Baudrillard writes: "The proliferation of technical gadgetry inside the house, beneath it, around it, like drips in an intensive care ward, the TV, stereo, and video which provide communication with the beyond, the car (or cars) that connect one up to that great shoppers' funeral parlor, the supermarket, and lastly, the wife and children, as glowing symptoms of success . . . everything here testifies to death having found its own ideal home." See Jean Baudrillard, *America* (New York, 1990). In addition, Paul Virilio states: "Where once the polis inaugurated a political theater, with its agora and its forum, now there is only a cathode-ray screen, where the shadows and specters of a community dance amid their processes of the disappearance of urbanism, the last image of and urbanism without urbanity. This is where tact and contact give way to televisual impact." See Paul Virilio, *Lost Dimension* (New York, 1991).

11. Carlo Aymonino states: "The character (or meaning) of a city is related to the degree of overlaying of spatial and interpretive elements, to the point in which they become indispensable to each other. This indispensability may only result in a 'judgement' if one reinterprets each time all the elements in the game; and to reinterpret means to plan . . . from this view point, the problems of 'insertion' and the more generic one of the 'environment' do not exist any more. What remains is the problem of more or less formally completed architectural complexes and urban sectors." Carlo Aymonino, "L'edificio e L' ambiente; premesse alla progettazione", lectures at the Corso di composizione dell' IUAV (Venezia, 1967): 20–21.

12. "The airplane is the product of close selection. The lesson of the airplane lies in the logic which governed the statement of the problem and its realization. The problem of the house has not yet been stated. Machinery contains in itself the factor of economy, which makes for selection. The house is a machine for living in." Le Corbusier, *Towards a New Architecture* (New York, 1960 ed.): 100.

13. "The house, the street, the town, are points to which human energy is directed: they should be ordered, otherwise they counteract the fundamental principles round which we revolve; if they are not ordered, they oppose themselves to us, they thwart us, as the nature all around us thwarts us, though we have striven with it, and with it begin each day a new struggle." Le Corbusier, *City of Tomorrow and Its Planning* (New York, 1929): 15.

14. Foucault states: "Order is, at one and the same time, that which is given in things as their inner law, the hidden network that determines the way they confront one another, and also that which has no existence except in the grid created by a glance, an examination, a language; and it is only in the blank spaces of this grid that order manifests itself in depth as though already there, waiting in silence for the moment of its expression." Michel Foucault, *The Order of Things: An Archaeology of the Human Sciences* (London, 1966).

Reprinted from *RE: American Dream*, (New York: Princeton Architectural Press, 1995): 40–54.

Mackey Apartments

Rather than statically preserving this historic building as a singular memory of its past life, COA's intention for the renovation of the Mackey apartments by Rudolph Schindler (1939) embraces the concept of Renovation Through Transformation. The renovation itself, responding to the new program of the MAK Center for Art and Architecture, openly acknowledges the building's new mission, accepting changes in information technology, program, and building use as well as providing an atmosphere that assists the visiting artists and support staff to work toward the production of contemporary art and architecture. Besides providing living quarters and studios for artists, the project houses the MAK Archives in the double-height penthouse apartment. The archives, which are run by a small staff, will occasionally host symposia and exhibitions of the artists' work.

A large part of the work consisted of new furniture for the apartments. To clearly define the extent of the work, COA designed or selected pieces that would not be confused with the furniture designs of Schindler. Using proportion and material selection as criteria, COA produced furniture that is strong, lightweight, durable, and supports the lifestyle of the inhabitants.

Mackey Apartments

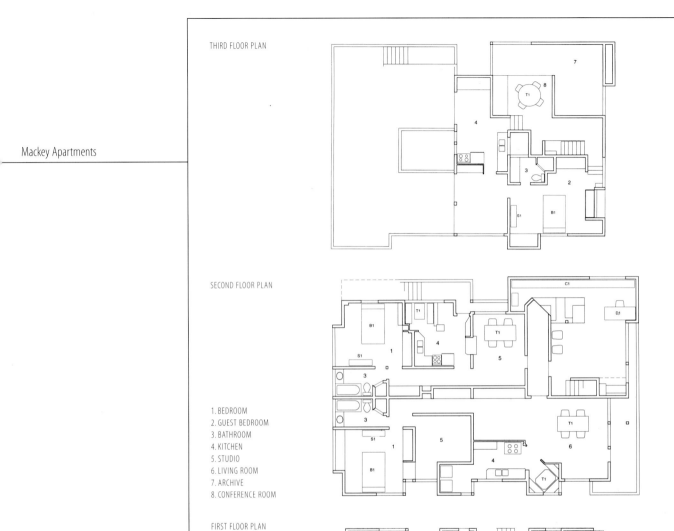

THIRD FLOOR PLAN

SECOND FLOOR PLAN

1. BEDROOM
2. GUEST BEDROOM
3. BATHROOM
4. KITCHEN
5. STUDIO
6. LIVING ROOM
7. ARCHIVE
8. CONFERENCE ROOM

FIRST FLOOR PLAN

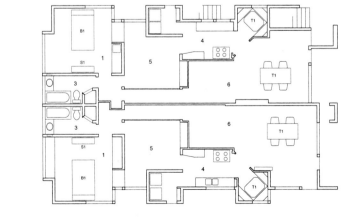

B1. BEDROOM
C1. CREDENZA
DI. DESK
SI. BENCH
T1. TABLE

Custom made furniture acts as equipment to respond to use within each space, and acts as a foil to the original building.

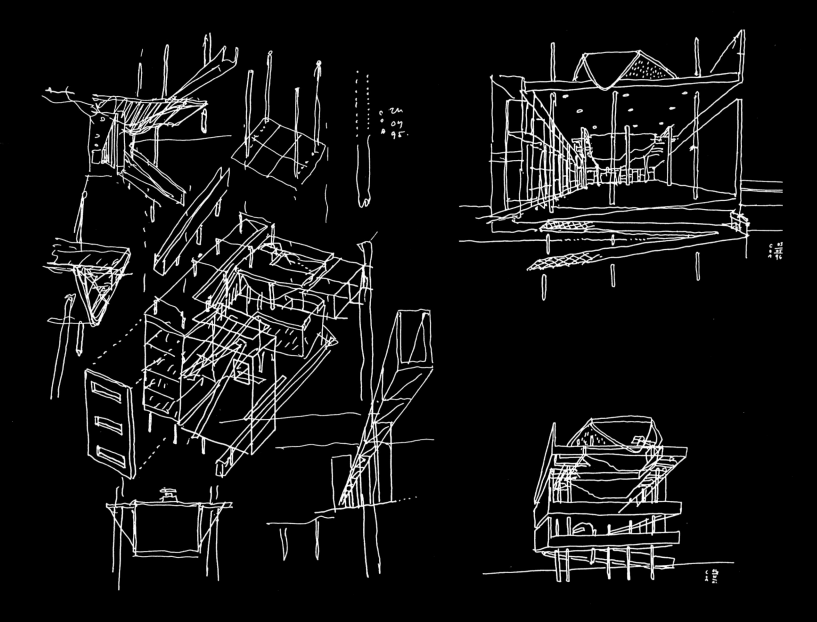

In Progress ▶

Maison Outil

This project presents a set of concerns similar to those of the residence in Pacific Palisades—the modification of the generic tract house.

On a 7500-square-foot (675-square-meter) lot located in Los Angeles, COA designed a 1700-square-foot (153-square-meter) addition using a free plan arrangement of living areas, painting studio space, sleeping quarters, and a home office. A courtyard serves as an exterior room.

As in the Pacific Palisades residence, the addition departs from the character of the existing residence while maintaining geometric relationships. The intervention consists of three discreet programmatic volumes united through the incorporation of Le Corbusier's anthropocentric numerical progression, Le Modulor. The project, although a singular object, aligns itself ideologically with a frame of mind for living in mass-produced houses. It is a rigorous response to the problem of dwelling "clearly stated." The intentional disposition of the tectonic/programmatic volumes to the void of the courtyard creates a close relationship between exterior leisure/gathering spaces and the interior spaces.

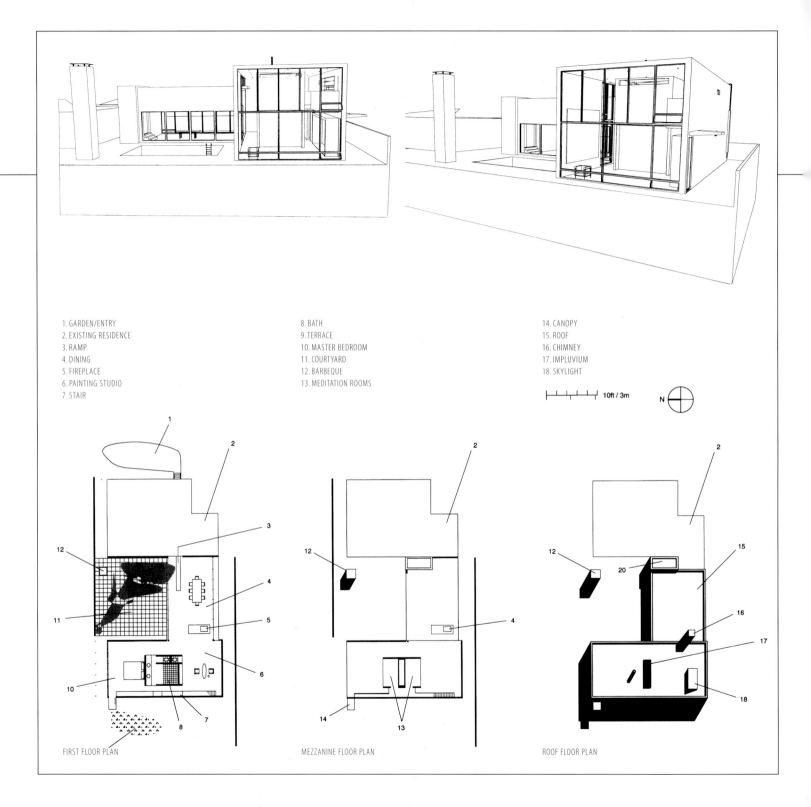

1. GARDEN/ENTRY
2. EXISTING RESIDENCE
3. RAMP
4. DINING
5. FIREPLACE
6. PAINTING STUDIO
7. STAIR

8. BATH
9. TERRACE
10. MASTER BEDROOM
11. COURTYARD
12. BARBEQUE
13. MEDITATION ROOMS

14. CANOPY
15. ROOF
16. CHIMNEY
17. IMPLUVIUM
18. SKYLIGHT

10ft / 3m

N

FIRST FLOOR PLAN

MEZZANINE FLOOR PLAN

ROOF FLOOR PLAN

C-22

C-5

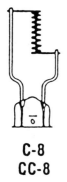

C-8
CC-8

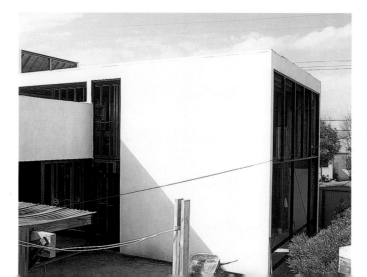

The interlocking volumes of living and sleeping areas form a private courtyard space with the existing house (top). Inside the painting studio, a skylight rotates out of the roof to capture north light. Like a tool, the house responds in a straightforward manner to the requirements and joys of living.

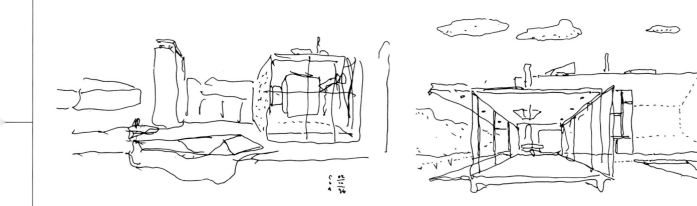

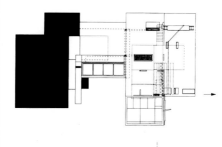
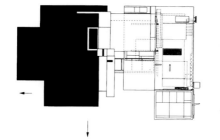
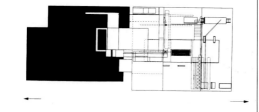

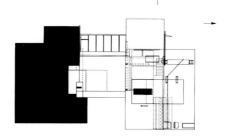
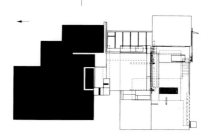
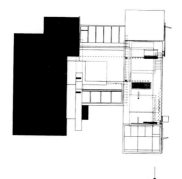

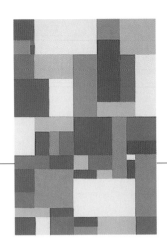

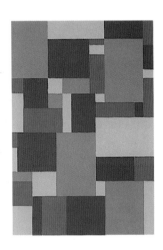

Le Corbusier's Modulor proportioning
system provided a basis for scaling
the building volumes and elements to
each other and to the human body,
resulting in a harmonious ensemble.
Color panel studies by COA (right).

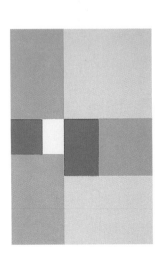

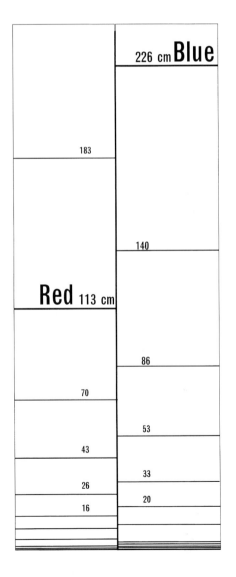

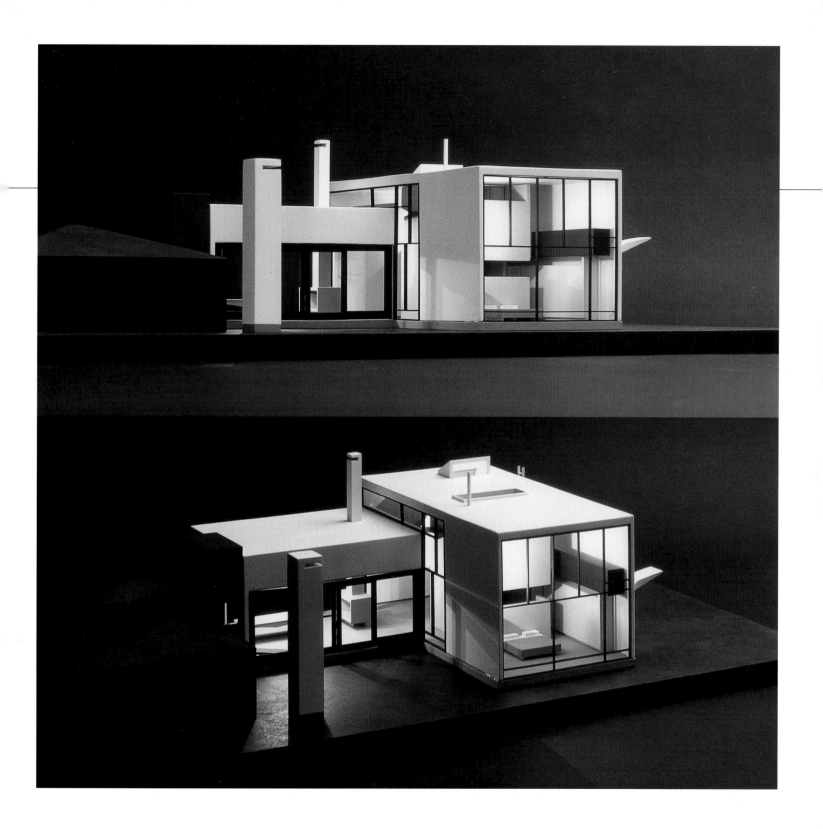

Villa Marisol

BAJA CALIFORNIA SUR, MEXICO

This 5000-square-foot (450-square-meter) villa, primarily a vacation retreat, sits on two acres of land in Baja California Sur, Mexico. Its only architectural context is a concrete and stone wall, part of a land division grid set up when the territory was established. A series of new walls organizes the program internally and implies a larger-scale relationship to the extraordinary view of water, sky, and the coastline's sand and rock.

Organizing the site as a mapped entity creates a dialectic between architecture and nature. The site parti is a cartesian theater punctuated by a point grid blanketing the entire site, around which a frame is constructed. A stone-walled courtyard rises to a height of 12 feet (3.7 meters) above sea level and locates the piano nobile at this surrogate horizon line.

The main house defines one edge while the gate house occupies the opposite corner. Constructed of poured-in-place concrete, the villa anchors itself to the perimeter wall and proclaims the difference between the striated domain within and the smooth, unmapped nature beyond. The center of the site is reserved for a labyrinthine garden.

The villa consists of four interrelated levels:
1) The ground level is a field of piloti with guest quarters, open gardens, and shaded outdoor dining spaces.
2) The piano nobile is a free plan distribution of living, dining, and kitchen areas.
3) The second floor contains three bedrooms and bathrooms with outdoor courtyard spaces.
4) The third floor is topped by a roof garden and changing room/bathroom.

Movement through the site/building is orchestrated through the framing and construction of paired opposites. Precise relationships clarify the fundamental relationships between ground plane and tectonic plane, between immediate ground and horizon, and between the site's center and its perimeter edge threshold.

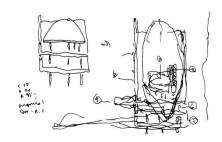

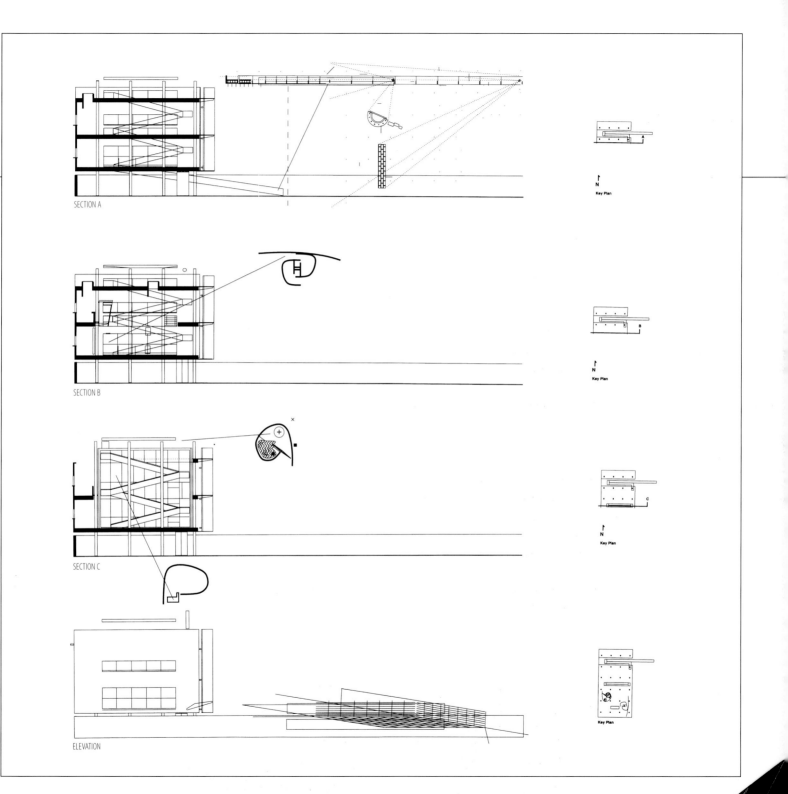

SECTION A

Key Plan

SECTION B

Key Plan

SECTION C

Key Plan

ELEVATION

Key Plan

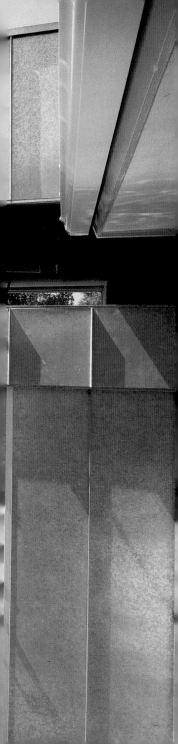

List of Works and Credits

THE ABSOLUTE AND AUTONOMOUS OBJECT
Architectural League of New York; 1986
Award: Young Architects Forum 1986
Project Team: Central Office of Architecture Partners
Photographer: Central Office of Architecture

RECOMBINANT IMAGES
Los Angeles Forum for Architecture and Urban Design;
1989 Publication No. 4
Project Team: Central Office of Architecture Partners
Photographer: Central Office of Architecture

PACIFIC PALISADES RESIDENCE
Pacific Palisades, California; 1989
Client: Name withheld at client's request
Project Team: Central Office of Architecture Partners
Contractor: Roman Janczak Construction
Structural Engineer: Miguel Castillo (MAC)
Mechanical/Electrical: In—Floor
Art: Blake Summers
Photographers: Tom Bonner (pages 25, 28-29, 30 top, 32, 33, 34, 35, 128); Central
Office of Architecture (pages 6, 24, 27, 30 bottom)

LAGUNA BEACH RESIDENCE
Laguna Beach, California; 1988
Client: Name withheld at client's request
Project Team: Central Office of Architecture Partners
Contractor: Surfside Builders
Structural Engineer: Miguel Castillo (MAC)
Art: Jim Dine, Blake Summers
Photographers: Central Office of Architecture (pages 39, 42, 43, 44, 45, 47);
Benny Chan (pages 37, 40-41)

GROUP ONE OFFICES
Los Angeles, California; 1987
Client: Group One Productions
Project Team: Central Office of Architecture Partners
Contractor: Central Office of Architecture
Photographer: Central Office of Architecture

LOS ANGELES AND THE CURSE OF BIGNESS
Los Angeles, California; 1988
Project Team: Central Office of Architecture Partners
Photographer: Central Office of Architecture
Aerial photograph of downtown Los Angeles (page 58) courtesy of Western
Economic Research Company, Inc.

SILVERLAKE RESIDENCE
Los Angeles, California; 1993
Client: Miyoshi Barosh
Project Team: Central Office of Architecture Partners
Contractor: Roman Janczak Construction
Photographer: Central Office Of Architecture

RECYCLING L.A.
Los Angeles, California; 1990
Project Team: Central Office of Architecture Partners
Photographer: Central Office of Architecture (page 64); Benny Chan (page 66)

BRIX RESTAURANT
Los Angeles, California; 1991
Client: Rick E. Figs
Project Team: Central Office of Architecture Partners
Contractor: Tom Listerud
Structural Engineer: William Koh
Mechanical/Electrical: Hooshang Mosaffari, P.E., Rahim Pavan
Photographers: Tom Bonner (pages 16, 68, 69, 73, 74-75, 76, 77); Central Office of
Architecture (pages 70, 71)

GLENDALE RESIDENCE
Glendale, California; 1989
Client: Lawrence and Debra McGinty–Poteet
Project Team: Central Office of Architecture Partners
Assistant: Jeff Schell
Structural Engineer: William Koh
Photographer: Benny Chan

DYNAMIC OF THE METROPOLIS
Los Angeles, California; 1990
Client: School of Architecture and Urban Design, University of California
Los Angeles (UCLA)
Project Team: Central Office of Architecture Partners
Collection of the San Francisco Museum of Modern Art
Photographers: Benny Chan (pages 7, 87, 88-89); UCLA Archives (page 86)

RESTROOM PROTOTYPE
Los Angeles, California; 1990
Client: City of Los Angeles Department of Parks and Recreation
Project Team: Central Office of Architecture Partners
Assistants: Benny Chan, Arturo Moreno, Sergio Ortiz, Luis Herrera, Sanam Simzar
Photographer: Central Office of Architecture

HAWKES PHOTOGRAPHY
Los Angeles, California; 1993
Client: William Hawkes
Project Team: Central Office of Architecture Partners
Photographer: William Hawkes

RE: AMERICAN DREAM
New Urban Housing Prototypes for Los Angeles; 1992
Project Team: Central Office of Architecture Partners, David Leclerc
Photographers: Tom Bonner (pages 102-103, 110); Central Office of Architecture
(pages 99, 108 bottom left, 109); Benny Chan (page 108 top left)
Film stills of *Mon Oncle* by Jacques Tati (pages 101, 104) courtesy of Panoramic
Films, Colombes, France, and Sophie Tatischeff.
Text and selected photographs reprinted from *RE: American Dream*, courtesy of
Princeton Architectural Press, New York, 1995.

MACKEY APARTMENTS
Los Angeles, California; 1995
Client: MAK Center for Art and Architecture, Peter Noever, Director
Project Team: Central Office of Architecture Partners.
Assistants: Fadi Hakim, Davis Marques
Contractor: Central Office of Architecture
Structural Engineer: Gordon Polon
Photographer: Central Office of Architecture

MAISON OUTIL
Encino, California; 1995–(in progress)
Client: Roman Janczak, Joan Jaeckel
Project Team: Central Office of Architecture Partners
Assistant: Fadi Hakim
Contractor: Roman Janczak Construction
Structural Engineer: Gordon Polon
Mechanical/Electrical: Roman Janczak Construction
Art: Central Office of Architecture
Photographer: Central Office of Architecture

VILLA MARISOL
Baja California, Mexico; 1996–(in progress)
Client: Sra. Angelina Berbeyer
Project Team: Central Office of Architecture Partners

ADDITIONAL PHOTOGRAPHIC CREDITS
Tom Bonner (page 12 right)
Central Office of Architecture (pages 8, 9, 10, 11, 12 left, 14)
Susan Middleton and David Liittschwager (page 15)

The COA offices: (left to right) Eric A.
Kahn, Ron Golan, Russell N. Thomsen.

ACKNOWLEDGMENTS

We wish to thank Rockport Publishers and the members of the board for their interest and support of our work. We extend our special thanks to Michael Rotondi for his unwavering support and inspired foreword essay, and to David Leclerc for his invaluable contributions as both critic and collaborator to contextualize the work.

We would also like to extend our gratitude to Aaron Betsky of the San Francisco Museum of Modern Art, the Architectural League of New York, certain faculty at the Southern California Institute of Architecture, Reverb, and Lorraine Wild, all of whom supported us early on. In addition, we appreciate the opportunity to have worked with many individuals too numerous to name at Arizona State University, Woodbury University, and the Royal Danish Academy of Art in Copenhagen, whose critical dialogue contributed to the development of our thinking.

As for those who have assisted in the production of our work, a heartfelt thanks to Benny Chan, Doron Drexler, Carlos Gomez, Fadi Hakim, Luis Herrera, Vince Lee, Doug Macaraeg, Davis Marques, Ross Miller, Arturo Moreno, Sergio Ortiz, Jason Payne, Jeff Schell, and Sanam Simzar for their energy and patience.

We wish to express our gratitude to Oscar Riera Ojeda for his continuing support and keen eye in the careful production of this book. To Patricia, Isaac, and Masako, thank you for your support and inspiration. Finally, to L-C, who continues to clarify and inspire.

Dedication:

To our parents,

     Simcha and Maxine

     Benjamin and Jean

     Roger and Doris